Understanding Expert Systems

Written by: Louis E. Frenzel, Jr.

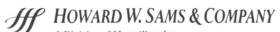 HOWARD W. SAMS & COMPANY
A Division of Macmillan, Inc.
4300 West 62nd Street
Indianapolis, Indiana 46268 USA

International Standard Book Number: 0-672-27065-X
Library of Congress Catalog Card Number: 87-72206

Acquisitions Editor: Greg Michael
Manuscript Editor: Don MacLaren
Cover Art: Diebold Glascock Advertising Inc.
Cover Photography: Castle Productions, Inc.
Components Courtesy of: WRTV, Indianapolis
Illustrator: Don Clemons
Indexer: Sandi Schroeder
Compositor: Shepard Poorman Communications Corp.

Printed in the United States of America

Table of Contents

Preface

A new kind of computer software has captured the interest and imaginations of a lot of computer users. It's called expert systems. Like many developments in the computer field, expert systems have exhibited many of the characteristics of short-term fads, but now they appear to be a genuinely new type of computer software that will show long-term growth and stability as the technology develops.

Over the past several years, the interest in expert systems has grown tremendously. R&D in expert systems dates back to the mid-1960s, but only in the last several years has the technology become practical. Expert systems are a kind of artificial intelligence software. Artificial intelligence is that part of the computer industry attempting to make computers work more like a human mind. Instead of giving computers repetitive data processing operations to perform, AI researchers are showing computers how to think and reason, enabling computers to solve a wide range of problems.

This book is written for those of you who wish to learn more about expert systems. It should satisfy your curiosity about expert systems and help you determine their impact on you. This book will tell you what expert systems are, how they work, and where they find the greatest application. With this book, you can start to develop your own simple expert systems.

The book is arranged like a textbook. Each chapter starts by saying what it will cover, ends by reviewing what it has covered, and includes a short quiz. Like other books in this series, this book builds understanding step-by-step. Try to master each chapter before moving on to the next.

LF

Expert Systems: The Big Picture

ABOUT THIS CHAPTER

This book is about expert systems, a contemporary type of software that is making computers more useful than ever before. In this first chapter, we introduce expert systems, explain what they are, and what they do. You will discover that expert systems are a special type of artificial intelligence, which itself is a special class of software. To understand expert systems, you need to know about artificial intelligence (AI), and so this chapter provides a basic background in AI techniques. Finally, we'll walk you through an actual consultation with an expert system on the computer. In this way, you'll get a feel for what this type of software can do for you.

EXPERT SYSTEMS DEFINED

Expert systems embody the knowledge of one or more experts.

Where do you go to get help in solving a complex problem? What do you do when you need detailed information on a highly technical subject? Where do you get the nitty-gritty information necessary to do your job competently or to make a particularly tough decision? People in situations like these often go to a person who is considered an expert in the relevant area. By going directly to a person who has in-depth knowledge of the subject, you can get a quick solution to your problem, find the information that you need, or make your difficult decision.

What Is an Expert?

Experts are specialists in a narrow field of interest who perform problem-solving and decision-making in their field.

An expert is a person who has considerable knowledge of a particular field. In artificial intelligence terminology, a person with a strong knowledge of a specific area is known as a "domain expert." This considerable knowledge is acquired through formal and informal learning as well as experience. Experts use their knowledge broadly to solve a wide range of problems. Their extensive experience makes them extremely valuable to their employers; experts can solve problems quickly and make good decisions quickly.

If you aren't an expert but require the expert's knowledge to do your job, you may be able to tap an available expert's knowledge. Then you can solve the problem, make the decision, or otherwise perform a task. The key to your success, though, is gaining access to the expert and his or her knowledge.

Experts are a rare commodity; because there are few of them, they are typically in great demand. As a result, experts are often overworked and spread too thin, and you may not be able to get access to an expert when you need one. If the expert is not available, what happens? Do you put your problem or decision on hold or do you take your best shot at it? The answer depends upon the situation. The point here is that to do your job in a timely manner you must have access to the knowledge and information you require. Without the expert, the job may go undone or be done late or wrong.

An expert system is a clone of a human expert.

One solution to this dilemma is to have multiple experts. When this isn't possible, a clone of your expert would be just as suitable. And if you think that cloning an expert is not possible, think again. An expert system is simply a software clone of your expert.

An expert system replicates expert knowledge in a discipline and makes it available on a computer so that you may tap it when you need it.

An expert system packages the knowledge of one or more experts in a specific domain into software that can operate on virtually any computer. When you need an expert you call it up on the computer. Even if the domain is a complex one, you can achieve the same result with an expert system that the expert could achieve faced with the same problem. Having an expert system at your disposal will not make you an expert, but it enables you to do some, possibly all, of the work of the expert who is in short supply.

Benefits of Expert Systems

Improve Productivity

Expert systems can potentially improve productivity, save time and money, preserve valuable knowledge, and improve our learning and understanding.

The principal benefit of expert systems is that they improve productivity. Essentially, *productivity* refers to the amount of work produced in a given period of time. High productivity means lots of work done in a short period of time. Expert systems can often improve productivity because they put valuable knowledge at your fingertips so that it may be applied when needed, helping you get the job done more quickly or permitting you to accomplish more work in the same time.

Expert systems also save time and money. With knowledge readily available, problems may be solved when they occur and decisions can be made quickly. Further, expert systems can save money by solving problems in a timely manner and by avoiding costly mistakes and bad decisions. Expert systems can improve not only the quantity of work, but also its quality.

Preserve Valuable Knowledge

The knowledge of an expert is an extremely valuable commodity. In most cases, it has taken the expert considerable time and effort to acquire that expertise. Formal education and many years of experience go into the making of an expert. While it is difficult to put a price on an expert's knowledge, it obviously has value, particularly to an employer. That knowledge is useful in day-to-day operations and without it serious problems would arise. Losing an expert is usually a catastrophe.

Expert systems allow you to preserve the expert's valuable knowledge. The expert becomes your prime resource in developing an expert system that embodies his or her knowledge and perhaps that of others. Should the expert leave, his or her knowledge can still be used if it has been acquired and appropriately packaged into a usable expert system. The result can be a competitive advantage of great benefit.

Expert systems allow an expert's highly valuable knowledge to be saved and encapsulated as software that can be widely disseminated. That knowledge is not lost if the expert is. Until recently, most organizations had no way to save their expert's knowledge. Now they do.

Expert systems provide a new way to preserve knowledge. Experts often write books that help capture what they know. Books tend to be more theoretical than practical, though, and often the ability to apply knowledge cannot be taught in a book so the application of the knowledge is left to the reader. Expert systems provide a unique format for preserving certain types of knowledge. To create an expert system, the essence of the problems to be solved is determined and the exact kind of knowledge needed to solve those problems is obtained and programmed into the system. The result is software that directly solves the problems.

Improve Understanding and Learning

Expert systems also help us understand how an expert goes about solving a problem or otherwise applying knowledge. In creating an expert system, the developer attempts to determine exactly what knowledge is required and how it is used. Often experts don't understand exactly how they go about solving problems. Experts often take their knowledge for granted and never analyze the way they apply it. But to create the expert system, the developer must discover such details. This leads to a better understanding of how the human mind reasons.

Expert systems can also improve learning. An individual using an expert system to solve problems on a regular basis will eventually become quite familiar with the subject matter. If sufficient experience is gained in using the expert system on a variety of problems, the user's performance may approach that of an expert.

KNOWLEDGE: THE HEART OF ALL EXPERT SYSTEMS

The heart of all expert systems is knowledge. As a result, they are often referred to as knowledge-based systems.

As you have no doubt gleaned from the foregoing, the key to every expert system is knowledge. Because knowledge forms the core of expert systems, expert systems are often referred to as knowledge systems or knowledge-based systems. The field of expert systems is concerned with ways to acquire knowledge from human experts and represent it in a form compatible with computers. The computers perform a kind of knowledge processing when the user taps the knowledge.

What Is Knowledge?

Knowledge is acquired understanding.

Knowledge is human understanding of a field of interest that has been acquired through education and experience. Knowledge implies learning, awareness, and familiarity with one or more subjects. Knowledge is made up of ideas, concepts, facts and figures, theories, procedures, relationships among these, and ways to apply these to practical problem-solving.

In some applications, the knowledge for an expert system can come straight out of a textbook, a policy and procedures manual, or another source. By reformatting the knowledge in existing documentation, an expert system can be created.

For many applications, heuristic knowledge acquired through real-world experience is best for practical problem-solving.

However, in most applications the kind of knowledge that works best in an expert system and proves to be the most valuable is *heuristic* knowledge. Heuristic knowledge is practical real-world understanding. It includes all of those tricks of the trade, rules of thumb, and gimmicks that an expert uses to solve problems. Heuristic knowledge is not textbook or classroom knowledge, but instead it is that kind of knowledge that has been acquired through years of experience and exposure to a wide variety of problems and situations. Heuristic knowledge lets experts solve problems quickly primarily because they know what works and what doesn't work in a given situation. The trick in expert system development is to identify heuristic knowledge, extract it from the expert, and represent it in the computer.

Information Is Not Knowledge

Information is facts and figures. Knowledge is understanding those facts and figures.

Don't confuse information and knowledge. While the two terms are often used interchangeably, the differences are important. Information is primarily facts and figures. In other words, information is raw data that hasn't been interpreted. Knowledge, on the other hand, is an *understanding* of the information based on analysis, a realization of its importance, and its applications. There is a tremendous amount of information in this world but much less understanding of that information. John Naisbitt, in his 1984 book *Megatrends,* says it well: "We are drowning in information but starved for knowledge."

Most agree that we live in an information society. Much of our effort goes into developing, packaging, and disseminating information in some way. Regardless of your work, you are, in most cases, a generator of information which you pass on to others. You are also a user of information. An enormous amount of information is developed and communicated daily. Undoubtedly you have felt the effect of this information glut. You receive many forms of information in many different ways. It may be a memo that arrives in the interoffice mail, a catalog that comes in the mail, a news broadcast on radio, an educational video, or a computer spreadsheet. Magazines, newspapers, proposals, reports, and other documents make up the information sources in our lives. It is difficult to know just what information sources exist much less to acquire and use them all. A subtle part of your job is in knowing the information sources and using them selectively to solve your problems.

Expert systems help you deal with info overload by translating information into usable knowledge.

Expert systems provide one more way to help you get control of this information blizzard. Expert systems package knowledge. That knowledge comes from information that has been analyzed and understood. A subject matter expert can boil down the essential knowledge into a concise form that can be put into an expert system for use in practical problem-solving.

Information is what most computers work with. The spreadsheets, data bases, word processing documents, and other kinds of information are readily processed by computers. Computers are designed to store massive amounts of information and make it easy to retrieve. Computers also "crunch numbers"; that is, they alleviate the burdensome task of dealing with repetitive, difficult, time-consuming, error-prone mathematical calculations. Information is readily stored in computers because numbers and text can be easily coded into binary form suitable for computer storage and manipulation. The big problem in developing expert systems is representing knowledge rather than information in a computer. The field of expert systems is largely devoted to finding better ways to represent knowledge in a computer. You'll learn about the most popular methods later in this book.

AN INTRODUCTION TO ARTIFICIAL INTELLIGENCE (AI)

We said earlier that expert systems are a type of artificial intelligence. Now that you know what an expert system is and what it does, it is time to take a look at AI, the broad field from which expert systems are derived.

AI is that "weird" part of the computer field concerned with making computers more intelligent and hence more useful.

AI is that area of computer science concerned with making computers smarter. More specifically, AI is that collection of techniques that permit a computer to mimic the human mind. AI research attempts to discover ways to make a computer think and reason like a human. In general, the goal of AI is to make computers more powerful and useful by making them emulate functions of the brain. Standard data processing solutions do not work with some kinds of problems. But with AI these problems can be tackled. In addition, AI helps make computers easier to use, enabling more people to use them. AI has the potential for making computers as easy to use as a telephone.

Can a computer really think? Like many who encounter AI, you may wonder whether it is possible to construct an electronic machine that will understand and reason like a human. The answer to the question is a qualified yes. Computers can be programmed to think in a limited way and to perform reasoning operations that a human might ordinarily do. On the other hand, it is not possible to perfectly duplicate the incredibly complex human brain. It is doubtful that a machine with intelligence approaching that of a human will ever be built. Like most other humans, you will probably say "thank goodness" for that. You don't have to worry about being replaced by a computer, but most likely you will have an AI computer to which you can delegate some work or tap to get help with other work.

It is not the goal of AI to replace humans with smart computers, but to make computers smarter so they become a more powerful tool and thus more valuable and broadly useful.

The ability to duplicate limited forms of human thinking is desirable. Computers are tools that we use to help us do our work. Computers let us perform many operations faster and easier than we could do them ourselves with conventional mental and manual methods. In general, computers improve our productivity and let us do things that we could not do ordinarily. AI takes computers one step farther, allowing them to do more mental operations than they could using conventional data processing techniques. The result is a more useful machine. With AI, computers become a different kind of tool that can be applied in new and useful ways.

INTELLIGENCE AND WISDOM

Intelligence is the ability of a person to think or reason. It is the capability of acquiring knowledge and applying it. Humans have native intelligence and can build or improve upon it. Machines can also have intelligence, at least on a limited scale. That intelligence is given it by humans, however, and its quality depends upon how it is represented in and used by the machine.

Wisdom embodies intelligence but also an understanding of what is right, wrong, true, false, and of lasting value. A wise person is learned and experienced. Wisdom also implies common sense and good judgement. Computers may have limited forms of intelligence, but only humans can have wisdom.

Conventional vs. AI Computing

Expert systems and other forms of AI are software that can be made to work on almost any digital computer.

Artificial intelligence and expert systems are software. They are a collection of programs that make a computer think, reason, and apply the knowledge stored in them. Computers are general-purpose boxes of electronic components that are designed to process information in some way. By themselves, they are worthless. But given appropriate software, computers become those powerful tools that many have learned to love or hate.

Most computers use what we can call conventional software. These are the programs that solve math problems, manipulate data bases, compute spreadsheets, spell-check a document, among other functions. AI software is different from these. It uses a totally new approach to solving a problem, called "symbolic processing," in which the computer is given reasoning capability that simulates what a human might do. Let's examine the basic kinds of computing.

Conventional Computing

An algorithm describes ingredients and how to combine them, like a recipe.

Figure 1-1 lists most of the ways computers process data. Conventional software is used to perform all of these operations. To implement these functions, programs are written that tell the computer specifically what to do. The computer is given a step-by-step sequence called an "algorithm," which clearly defines the actions that must be taken to solve a given problem.

Figure 1-1.
How Conventional
Software Programs
Process Data on
Computer

1. STORE data such as facts, figures, text, etc. in files.
2. RETRIEVE data from files.
3. CALCULATE with data. Perform math operations, solve formulas, etc.
4. TRANSLATE data from one form to another.
5. SORT data by selecting desired items or rearranging their order.
6. EDIT data by making additions, deletions, or changes.
7. DECIDE amongst alternatives, reach conclusions.
8. MONITOR internal or external events and take action if specific conditions are met.
9. CONTROL internal or external devices.

To solve a conventional computer problem, a programmer first analyzes the problem to determine exactly what the inputs are and what the desired outputs should be. The programmer then comes up with an algorithm that processes the inputs to produce the output. That algorithm is a clearly defined incremental procedure that does the desired manipulation. The programmer then takes this algorithm and converts it into a sequential list of instructions, statements, or commands as defined by a programming language. In turn, that programming language produces the binary code that is stored in the computer memory. When executed, the program solves the problem exactly as specified.

Figure 1-2 shows a block diagram of a general-purpose digital computer and how the computer performs conventional computing. The algorithm is stored in the computer memory along with the data to be processed. The algorithm manipulates the input data to produce the desired output.

**Figure 1-2.
How Computer
Processes Conventional
Algorithmic Software**

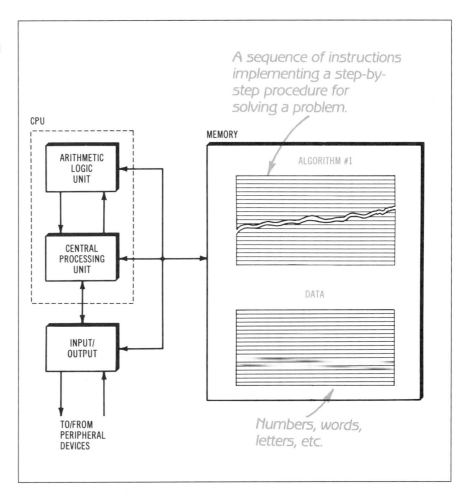

AI Computing

A symbol is something
that represents something
else.

AI, or symbolic, computing uses a totally different approach
to problem solving. It starts with knowledge of the domain. This
knowledge must be represented in a form that can be stored in a
computer. The knowledge is represented symbolically. A symbol is
nothing more than a word, letter, or number that you use to
represent objects, actions, and their relationships. These objects
can, of course, represent anything, including people, places, events,
and ideas. These symbols can be stored in the computer memory as
ASCII characters or strings. Through the use of symbols, you can
create a *knowledge base* which states various facts about the
objects, actions, or processes, and how all of them are interrelated.

The two main parts of any AI software are a knowledge base and an inferencing program.

Once the knowledge base has been created, a method must be devised to use it. Basically. a program is needed that will use the knowledge to reason and think in an effort to solve a particular problem. This kind of program is generally referred to as an "inferencing program," or "inferencing engine," which is designed to make decisions and judgements based upon the symbolic data in the knowledge base. The inferencing program accepts external inputs about the problem and then attempts to apply the available knowledge to its solution.

The inferencing program manipulates the symbolic information in the knowledge base through a process of search and pattern-matching. The inferencing program is provided with some initial inputs that provide sufficient information for the program to begin. Using these initial inputs, the inferencing program searches the knowledge base looking for matches. The search continues until a solution is found. The initial search may turn up a match that will, in turn, lead to another search and another match, and so on. The inferencing program performs a series of these searches that are chained together. This chain simulates a logical reasoning process.

The basic problem-solving approach of any AI program is search and pattern-matching.

All AI programs use this search and pattern-matching approach, looking for links and relationships. This process may solve the problem satisfactorily; in some cases, though, the problem may not be solved at all. If insufficient knowledge is available or insufficient input data is given, symbolic computing may not be able to solve the problem. This is in contrast to conventional computing where an algorithm always produces a solution if given input data to process. However, when enough input is provided and a good knowledge base exists, very satisfactory solutions usually result from symbolic computing. The effect is as if a human had solved the problem.

The inferencing program is implemented with algorithms that define the search and pattern-matching techniques to be used on the symbolic knowledge base. It is these techniques that solve the problem, not the algorithms. The simplified block diagram of a digital computer in *Figure 1-3* shows how the knowledge base and inferencing programs are stored in memory.

AI software tells "what" but not "how."

Conventional software does procedural processing in which the algorithm details specifically how to solve the problem. AI software, including expert systems, does non-procedural processing. The program contains the "what" of the problem but not the "how." The "what" is the knowledge and any input data. But no procedure manipulates this "what" according to a step-by-step "how." Instead, through its search and matching processes, the inference program finds its own conclusion.

**Figure 1-3.
How Computer
Processes AI Software**

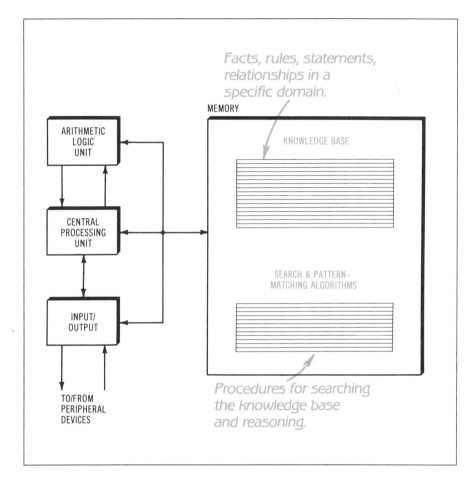

Applications of AI

Artificial intelligence can be applied to an incredibly wide range of problems. Any problem that doesn't lend itself to an algorithmic solution is a candidate for AI techniques. Since algorithms need specific pieces of data to solve the problem, many non-numerical problems containing uncertainty and ambiguity do not fit the algorithmic process. As it turns out, there are many situations in this world of ours that are disorganized or imperfect or that we lack complete information about. AI can deal with such problems, often producing a satisfactory solution.

Figure 1-4 shows the main applications categories of AI. Let's take a look at each of them.

**Figure 1-4.
Major Subfields of AI**

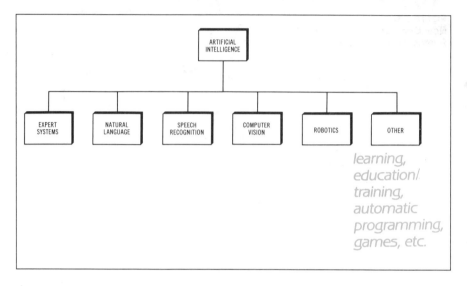

Natural Language Processing (NLP)

Natural language
processing programs
allow computers to
understand our language.

After expert systems, natural language processing is the most widely used AI application. Natural language refers to human language, as spoken and written. NLP programs accept natural language inputs, interpret and understand them, and produce natural language output.

Computers, of course, have many languages at different levels. At the lowest level, computers speak *binary*. The earliest computers were programmed in binary, but this was a tedious, error-prone process. Higher level languages were slowly developed to ease the programming problem. Assembly language and such higher level languages as BASIC, Fortran, COBOL, Pascal, and C, are now widely used to program computers. We have to learn to use such languages if the computer is going to respond correctly. Essentially, we must learn the computer's language in order to use it.

Wouldn't it be great if we could speak to the computer in our own language? Of course it would. With such a feature, virtually anyone could use a computer to accomplish useful work without learning the special language and procedures now required. NLP programs give us this facility.

Like all AI programs, natural language processing programs are made up of a knowledge base and an inferencing program. The knowledge base generally consists of a dictionary of words that the computer understands. When a natural language statement is typed

Book Mark

HOWARD W. SAMS & COMPANY
Excellence In Publishing

DEAR VALUED CUSTOMER:

Howard W. Sams & Company is dedicated to bringing you timely and authoritative books for your personal and professional library. Our goal is to provide you with excellent technical books written by the most qualified authors. You can assist us in this endeavor by checking the box next to your particular areas of interest.

We appreciate your comments and will use the information to provide you with a more comprehensive selection of titles.

Thank you,

Vice President, Book Publishing
Howard W. Sams & Company

SUBJECT AREAS:

Computer Titles:
☐ Apple/Macintosh
☐ Commodore
☐ IBM & Compatibles
☐ Business Applications
☐ Communications
☐ Operating Systems
☐ Programming Languages

Electronics Titles:
☐ Amateur Radio
☐ Audio
☐ Basic Electronics
☐ Electronic Design
☐ Electronic Projects
☐ Satellites
☐ Troubleshooting & Repair

Other interests or comments:

_____

_____

Name _____

Title _____

Company _____

Address _____

City _____

State/Zip _____

Daytime Telephone No. _____

A Division of Macmillan, Inc.
4300 West 62nd Street
Indianapolis, Indiana 46268 USA

27065

HOWARD W. SAMS
& COMPANY

Book Mark

HOWARD W. SAMS
& COMPANY

BUSINESS REPLY CARD

FIRST CLASS   PERMIT NO. 1076   INDIANAPOLIS, IND.

POSTAGE WILL BE PAID BY ADDRESSEE

HOWARD W. SAMS & CO.
ATTN: Public Relations Department
P.O. BOX 7092
Indianapolis, IN 46205

into the computer, the inferencing program examines it to determine whether the words within the input are understood. If they are, the desired action is initiated.

Great progress has been made over the years in developing NLP programs that understand complex natural language inputs. These programs are widely employed in a variety of applications. One of the most common is as a front-end, or interface, to another type of computer program, for instance, a data base management system (DBMS). Getting information out of a DBMS often requires complex programming to tell the computer exactly what information is required and how it should be output. Because of this complex programming problem, most users must ask a programmer for help. But with a natural language front-end, users can tap the DBMS themselves. Natural language front-ends are increasingly available on spreadsheets and expert systems and other frequently used programs.

Speech Recognition

Speech recognition systems mimic human hearing by recognizing and understanding the spoken word.

Closely related to natural language processing, speech recognition systems provide a fresh new way to use computers. NLP programs can understand text that is keyed in on a keyboard or is otherwise received in text format. In speech or voice recognition, the computer understands human speech. The computer input is a microphone which develops an electrical analog signal that is converted into binary numbers which an AI program can interpret. As with other AI programs, a search and pattern-matching approach is used. The binary input is compared to templates of previously stored input that are part of a knowledge base. If the input speech matches the template, in either complete words or sounds, recognition and understanding occur.

Computer Vision

Computer vision systems implement sight on the computer.

Computer vision systems use AI techniques to analyze and interpret visual information, replicating human sight. Typically the visual information is scanned by a TV camera and then converted into binary signals representing the visual image. The binary image is stored in the computer memory where it can be manipulated by the AI program. The AI program uses search and pattern-matching techniques to help identify objects and otherwise extract information from the visual data. A knowledge base containing templates of known shapes and patterns is used as a standard against which the inferencing program compares the binary inputs. If a match is obtained, identification and understanding results.

Computer vision systems have many applications. Most of the applications are for inspection and quality control in manufacturing, where they can replace human workers. They can also be used by the military and intelligence services to analyze satellite or aerial photographs.

Robotics

A robot is to the human body as AI is to the mind.

The field of artificial intelligence attempts to mimic the mental capabilities of humans. The field of robotics attempts to mimic the physical capabilities of humans. A robot is an electromechanical machine that attempts to duplicate certain functions of the human anatomy. The most widely used robotic device is a machine that simulates a human arm and hand. Known as manipulators, these robots are widely used in manufacturing operations to replace human workers at lifting and moving parts. Other robotic arms can weld, paint, and perform other manual operations. Because they never tire, robots perform much better than humans in such operations. Robots are also used in hazardous environments.

Most robots are controlled by an electronic controller or computer. Typically the computer is programmed with an algorithm that tells the arm specifically how to move. A problem with this approach is that the arm does exactly what it is told to do and nothing else. Items to be manipulated must be perfectly positioned with respect to the arm because it cannot make decisions and modify its operation to fit unusual conditions.

A smart robot can be created by using sensors for feedback and AI software to modify the control program.

The way to make robotic arms more useful then is to provide them with sensors and intelligence. By giving the robot the ability to sense its position or to see the item being worked upon, it can adjust to problems. Combining these sensors with AI software creates an intelligent robot that adapts to its surroundings. The result is greater productivity with fewer errors.

Other Applications

While these are the major application categories of AI, there are many smaller ones that don't neatly fit into one of these categories.

One smaller but important area of AI application is computer learning. Researchers are attempting to find ways to make the computer automatically learn from its experiences or from inputs provided. Learning is a key human capacity and AI researchers have yet to find an effective way to duplicate it. They are making progress, however, and incredible improvements in performance should be obtainable when learning computers become available.

AI is also being used in education and training. AI methods are being used to create a new form of computer-assisted instruction (CAI). In CAI, the computer becomes a tutor. Through computer screen and keyboard a student carries on a conversation with the computer. The computer may present information to be learned or respond to questions. Such CAI programs are now widely available, and, with AI, the programs can assess the student's strengths and weaknesses and adjust the content of the material being presented so that it focuses on the student's weaknesses.

Another application of AI is automatic programming, in which AI techniques are applied to the difficult task of creating software. While such programs may never replace programmers, they can help simplify and speed up the programming process. Even small improvements in programming productivity will be useful.

THE HARDWARE OF AI

Computers with large memories and fast processors are best at running AI programs, although AI and expert system software can run on almost any digital computer.

Artificial intelligence programs and expert systems can run on virtually any type of digital computer: mainframes, minicomputers, personal computers, and even dedicated microprocessors. However, AI and expert systems software often have special requirements. Many AI programs are large, requiring a tremendous amount of computer memory. Second, because of the way that the inferencing programs work, high-speed processing is usually required for satisfactory performance.

Most early AI programs and expert systems were implemented on mainframes or minicomputers that provided adequate memory and high processing speed. Many of today's AI programs and expert systems are still built on such large systems— one of the most popular for AI applications is the Digital Equipment Corporation VAX series of minicomputers. AI and expert systems can also be implemented on today's 16-bit and 32-bit personal computers which have huge amounts of memory and fast processing speeds.

AI and expert systems can also be implemented on dedicated microcontrollers. For example, those special computers buried in robotic control systems or those used for military weapons can now take advantage of AI techniques. An ideal application for expert systems is the on-board computer in a fighter aircraft which uses its intelligence to make decisions about radar images and weapons deployment. Computers that control factories or chemical processes can be given the intelligence to adapt to changing conditions and modify the control sequence or the process.

LISP Machines

A special type of computer that runs the popular AI language LISP is widely used for AI software.

The bulk of AI applications run on available digital computers but there is a special type of computer designed primarily for AI work. Called a LISP machine or AI workstation, this computer implements the LISP programming language in hardware. LISP is the most widely used AI language, and LISP machines make the development of AI software faster and easier than on conventional computers. A typical LISP machine is illustrated in *Figure 1-5*. While LISP machines cost more than conventional computers and are not as versatile, they are to be preferred in those applications where they are dedicated to large, high-performance AI programs written in LISP.

Parallel Processors

Most computers use a single CPU. Its high-speed operation allows the CPU to execute serially written programs rapidly. But many AI programs involving extended searches of huge knowledge bases severely tax even the fastest CPUs. To overcome this problem, a new kind of computer is emerging: the parallel processor.

Parallel processors use multiple CPUs to execute different parts of a program simultaneously to improve performance.

The parallel processor or computer uses two or more CPUs. The problem to be solved is divided into segments, each of which can run on a separate CPU. By partitioning the problem, the multiple CPUs can work on the various parts of the program simultaneously, thereby greatly improving performance. Parallel computers that improve performance on conventional problems are also being built. Such machines' performance approaches or equals that of the largest supercomputers but at a lower cost.

EXPERT SYSTEMS TODAY

Although expert systems are over ten years old, they are not widely understood.

Expert systems aren't new; the first ones were developed in the mid-1970s. But it wasn't until the early 1980s that expert systems and other forms of AI software began to emerge from the research laboratories and show up in practical applications.

Figure 1-5.
A LISP Machine, the TI
Explorer AI Workstation

While many expert systems are in use, they still represent only a tiny fraction of the total software being used today. Why has it taken so long for expert systems and other AI software to become useful?

Years of research and experimentation plus some technological improvements and software developments were needed to make AI practical.

Although the idea of artificial intelligence is no newer than that of the more widely understood digital computing, it has taken the some thirty years for those researching the field to identify and understand key principles. And it has taken time for the technology to progress to the point where the theories of AI could be implemented on an affordable basis. Today computing power is increasing while costs decrease; for less than $10,000 you can have a 32-bit personal computer on your desk that contains more memory and computing power than the mainframes of just a decade ago.

Major breakthroughs in software development have also helped make expert systems and other forms of AI practical. Because of the unusual requirements of AI software, special AI programming languages had to be developed. In addition, special software development programs have been devised to aid in the creation of expert systems. These programming tools enable individuals with no knowledge of programming to develop expert systems. This has made the development of expert systems faster and easier.

Now that appreciation for expert systems is growing, many major development programs are underway. The government, the military, and business and industry are investing millions of dollars in the development of expert systems and other AI software. As the hardware improves, as new software developments occur, and as additional experience is gained throughout the computer community, more expert systems will become available.

Most expert systems solve specific problems unique to the user organization. Few generic expert systems are available now.

Today most available expert systems are those that have been developed for dedicated in-house functions. These proprietary systems solve day-to-day problems unique to the organization. While no generic expert systems are available today, the many benefits of expert systems are proven. As a result, many generic expert systems will be developed.

USING A REAL EXPERT SYSTEM

What's it like to use an expert system? What do you do and what does the computer do? To give you a feel for this, we'll walk you through an actual session with a typical expert system.

Expert systems ask questions to get the initial input data they need to function.

Basically, you carry on a conversation with your computer. The computer presents information to you, provides menus of alternatives to select from, and asks questions. You respond by making choices, answering the questions, and entering data on the keyboard. This exercise provides the program the initial information it needs to define the problem or outline the scope of the questions to be answered or decisions to be made. Most expert systems know what they need, so they go about collecting this initial data at the beginning, leading you through the process. Once the expert system has enough information, it proceeds to solve the problem. It then presents its answers, conclusions, or recommendations.

This process is fast and simple. No computer expertise is necessary to use an expert system, and all those esoteric AI computing techniques are invisible.

A typical session with an expert system will illustrate this procedure. The expert system is a demonstration part of Texas Instrument's Personal Consultant expert system development program, which advises individuals on personal investments, specifically money market funds. The sequence of screens in *Figure 1-6* shows the entire process. The individual and situation are entirely hypothetical. The type in the second color indicates the user's response. After supplying the answer, the user presses the < RETURN-ENTER > key.

Figure 1-6.
Personal Consultant
Expert System
(Courtesy of
Texas Instruments, Inc.)

**Figure 1-6
Cont.**

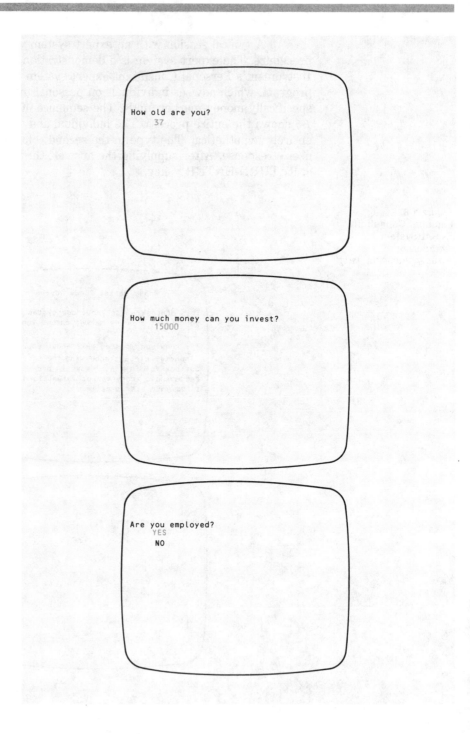

**Figure 1-6
Cont.**

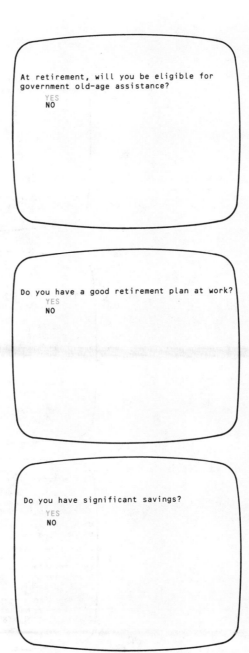

**Figure 1-6
Cont.**

```
What is the direction of short-term
interest rate movements?
     UP
     FLAT
     DOWN
```

```
The last time the central bank changed the
discount rate, did the rate increase or
decrease?
     INCREASE
     DECREASE
     UNKNOWN
```

```
Conclusions:

The client's name is as follows:  John David
The amount to invest is as follows:  15000
My recommendation is as follows:

When interest rates are not falling, a money
market fund is one of the best investments.

Since your risk profile indicates that you
can accommodate a certain degree of risk in
your investment strategy, invest in an
aggressive money market fund.  Select from
those funds offering the highest yields.

You can find a comparison of current yields
in the Money Market Funds column of the Wall
Street Journal. (80%)
```

FAMOUS EXPERT SYSTEMS

The expert systems described here are famous because of their impact on artificial intelligence. It took many years of research to develop these pioneer programs, which defined the format and operation of all expert systems today.

DENDRAL

DENDRAL is considered by many to be the first real expert system. It was created at Stanford University in the mid-1960s. Development on it and many successor programs continued through most of the 1970s. One of the most widely studied expert systems, the work done on DENDRAL has influenced the development of most expert systems.

The commercially available DENDRAL helps chemists determine the molecular structure of an unknown substance. Because of the incredible number of possible combinations of different substances, chemists find it difficult to infer the exact compound from test data. But, by using data gathered from a mass spectrometer, nuclear magnetic resonance measurements, and experimental chemical data, DENDRAL can reliably and quickly identify the compound.

MACSYMA

Developed at MIT, MACSYMA is designed to perform symbolic manipulation of mathematical expressions. MACSYMA was developed in the early 1970s and work on it has continued into the early 1980s. Able to perform differential and integral calculus symbolically, it helps scientists and engineers quickly solve complex problems that might take days or even months to complete by hand. MACSYMA also manipulates algebraic expressions and helps reduce them to their simplest form. Like DENDRAL, MACSYMA is commercially available and it is used regularly by scientists and engineers to speed up and simplify their complex mathematical work.

MYCIN

MYCIN is an expert system developed at Stanford for diagnosing and treating infectious blood diseases. It is one of the most widely studied expert systems because of its great success. MYCIN was one of the first expert systems to use production rules and to employ the backward-chaining inference method. *Production rules* are IF-THEN statements that express chunks of knowledge that are readily applied to problem-solving. *Backward-chaining* refers to the search method used by the computer to look through the production rules and find an appropriate solution. MYCIN also introduced the concept of certainty factors, permitting reasoning with uncertainty. A *certainty factor* is a number that indicates the confidence placed in the answer.

A major feature of MYCIN is that its rule base is completely separate from its inference program. This permits the MYCIN knowledge base to be discarded, creating empty MYCIN or EMYCIN. EMYCIN is the model after which the modern expert development *shells* are patterned.

PROSPECTOR

PROSPECTOR, built on the technology of MYCIN, is an expert system designed to help geologists locate valuable ore deposits. Its knowledge base, which is implemented with production rules and semantic networks, contains expertise on the geology of ore deposits and the classification of various types of rocks and minerals. Given data about a particular area, PROSPECTOR can estimate the chance of finding various types of mineral deposits. PROSPECTOR has had some unusual successes in locating large deposits of valuable ore. It was developed in the early to mid-1970s at SRI International.

XCON

XCON is an expert system designed to help technicians at Digital Equipment Corporation (DEC) configure minicomputer systems. DEC's popular VAX minicomputer systems are available in a wide variety of models with extensive features and options that can be selected by the customer. Because of the number of possible combinations, DEC employees were finding it hard to produce the correct system in which all the components worked together. XCON generates the desired configuration automatically when given the customer's requirements.

XCON, originally called R1, was developed at Carnegie-Mellon University in the late 1970s and was revised and updated by DEC in the early 1980s. Today it is a successful working program and an excellent example of how expert systems are saving large corporations time and money.

What Have We Learned?

1. An expert system is a kind of software that packages the knowledge of one or more experts into a form that others may use to solve problems in a specific domain.

2. The main benefits of expert systems are that they improve productivity, preserve valuable knowledge, and improve understanding and learning. They often save time and money because the expert knowledge is more readily available when needed.

3. Knowledge is understanding of a subject gained from formal learning and real-world experience. Data, or information, is facts and figures that have not been analyzed, codified, or understood.

4. Expert systems are a type of artificial intelligence. AI is that field of computer science devoted to making computers more useful by making them smarter.

5. AI software permits a computer to think and reason, thus duplicating in a limited way the human thought process.

6. AI software manipulates symbols that represent objects and their relationships. The basic problem-solving approach in AI is search and pattern-matching. Conventional software uses algorithms, step-by-step procedures that solve problems directly.

7. The two main parts of any AI software are (a) a knowledge base and (b) an inferencing program that applies the knowledge to solve a problem.

8. Other major AI applications are natural language processing, speech recognition, computer vision, and robotics.

9. AI software can run on almost any conventional digital computer including mainframes, minis, and PCs.

10. A special type of computer used in AI work is the LISP machine or AI workstation, which embodies the powerful programming language LISP.

11. Parallel processors, computers using multiple CPUs, are ideal for some AI problems since they partition problems into segments that are solved simultaneously, producing faster results.

12. Expert systems are used in business and government to solve specific problems.

Quiz for Chapter 1

1. Expert systems are:
   a. hardware.
   b. software.
   c. hardware plus software.
   d. human experts.

2. The primary element in an expert system is:
   a. facts and figures.
   b. reasoning capability.
   c. AI techniques.
   d. knowledge.

3. Which of the following is *not* a benefit of an expert system?
   a. Replaces expensive humans.
   b. Improves productivity.
   c. Saves time, lowers costs.
   d. Preserves valuable knowledge.

4. Knowledge is:
   a. information.
   b. everything that is known.
   c. learning and experience.
   d. facts and figures.

5. The kind of knowledge most useful in an expert system is called:
   a. heuristic.
   b. theoretical.
   c. recent.
   d. artificial.

6. Expert systems are also called:
   a. data processors.
   b. information manipulators.
   c. knowledge-based systems.
   d. decision programs.

7. The major goal of AI is to make computers:
   a. faster.
   b. cheaper.
   c. smaller.
   d. smarter.

8. AI computers are designed to:
   a. mimic human thinking and reasoning.
   b. duplicate human physical characteristics.
   c. execute conventional software faster.
   d. improve computer performance.

9. Conventional data processing programs solve problems by way of a(n):
   a. calculation.
   b. algorithm.
   c. symbol.
   d. translation.

10. The basic problem-solving approach of an AI program is:
    a. procedural analysis.
    b. table look-up.
    c. decision theory.
    d. search and pattern-matching.

11. The two main parts of any AI program are:
    a. symbols and tables.
    b. data and algorithms.
    c. knowledge base and inferencing program.
    d. input and output.

12. Expert systems and other AI programs can run on:
    a. mainframes.
    b. minicomputers.
    c. personal computers.
    d. all of the above.

13. To provide adequate performance while running an AI program, a computer must have:
    a. lots of memory.
    b. a fast processor.
    c. both a and b.
    d. none of the above.

14. A special kind of computer used only in AI work is called a(n):
    a. LISP machine.
    b. AI processor.
    c. 5th generation computer.
    d. parallel processor.

15. A subfield of AI concerned with understanding English is called:
    a. speech recognition.
    b. natural language processing.
    c. verbal cognition.
    d. optical character recognition.

16. Computer vision programs identify objects by:
    a. computing their size and location.
    b. using a TV camera.
    c. comparing their binary image to a prestored template.
    d. using photocells.

17. An intelligent robot is one that:
    a. is driven by a computer.
    b. has senses for feedback.
    c. uses an AI program.
    d. all of the above.

18. A new kind of computer that greatly improves the performance of AI and conventional software is called a:
    a. multiprocessor.
    b. parallel processor.
    c. LISP machine.
    d. optical processor.

19. Which of the following is *not* a research area in AI?
    a. Learning.
    b. Computer-aided instruction.
    c. Number theory.
    d. Automatic programming.

20. Most expert systems available today are:
    a. organization and job specific.
    b. totally generic.
    c. marginally useful.
    d. competently replacing human workers.

21. Developed in the 1960s, the first useful expert system is called:
    a. MYCIN.
    b. PROSPECTOR.
    c. DENDRAL.
    d. CADUCEUS.

22. Which expert system was the first to clearly separate the knowledge base and the inference engine?
  a. DENDRAL.
  b. MYCIN.
  c. MACSYMA.
  d. PROSPECTOR.

Types of Expert Systems

ABOUT THIS CHAPTER

In this chapter, we'll outline the types of expert systems in use and we'll examine the kinds of problems that expert systems solve best. When you complete this chapter, you'll know how expert systems are being used and you'll have a feel for whether an expert system might be of value to you.

EXPERT SYSTEM CONFIGURATIONS

There are a variety of ways that expert systems can be set up and used. These configurations include stand-alone, hybrid or embedded, linked, dedicated, and real-time systems.

Stand-Alone Systems

Stand-alone expert systems are pure AI and run by themselves on the computer.

A stand-alone expert system is one that runs by itself and fully occupies its host computer. The program is loaded from a floppy disk or transferred from a hard disk into the computer memory and then executed. Most of the expert systems that you will encounter will be of this type.

Hybrid Programs

Conventional and AI programs may be mixed to form embedded or integrated software.

Expert systems that are embedded in or integrated with algorithmic routines are called hybrid programs. The two main types of embedded or integrated systems are illustrated in *Figure 2-1*. In *Figure 2-1a*, an expert system is the main program but it has embedded in it algorithmic subroutines. To perform its problem-solving function, the expert system may need to perform some calculations or do other jobs best assigned to algorithmic routines. The algorithms are buried in the expert system software, which refers to them when necessary.

**Figure 2-1.
Two Kinds of Hybrid
Programs**

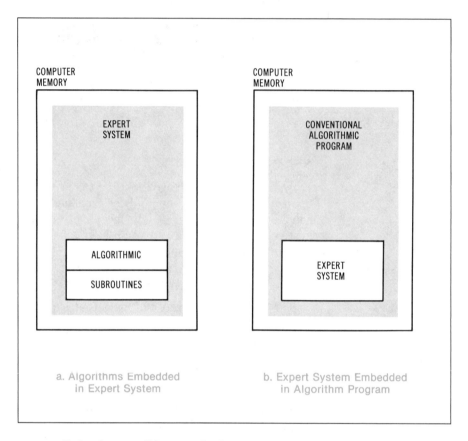

a. Algorithms Embedded
in Expert System

b. Expert System Embedded
in Algorithm Program

It is also possible to embed an expert system in a conventional algorithmic program, as *Figure 2-1b* shows. The main processing function is carried on by the conventional program, with occasional reference to the embedded expert system as the computing may require. For example, you could have an expert system that made critical accounting decisions based upon computations being made in a conventional general ledger or accounts payable program. The program would call the inferencing program of the expert system when such a decision was required.

Linked Software

Expert systems may be linked with one another or with conventional programs to get the inputs they need to solve problems.

Another form of mixed system is one that links conventional and AI programs or multiple expert systems. Commonly, the expert system requires input data from another source in order to solve the problem or make its decisions. Many expert systems are set up with links to external software packages such as spreadsheets or data base management systems. In this way, the expert system can tap the data stored in them. Many of the expert system development packages have built-in "hooks" to standard software packages that can provide this information.

It is also possible to link multiple expert systems. In large systems using a mainframe computer linked to personal computers, small local expert systems might run on the personal computers and a larger, related expert system run on the mainframe. These linked systems may exchange information with one another. Each of the smaller personal computer-based systems could make local decisions while the larger system could solve larger problems by calling on the smaller systems for inputs, as shown in *Figure 2-2.*

**Figure 2-2.
A Linked System**

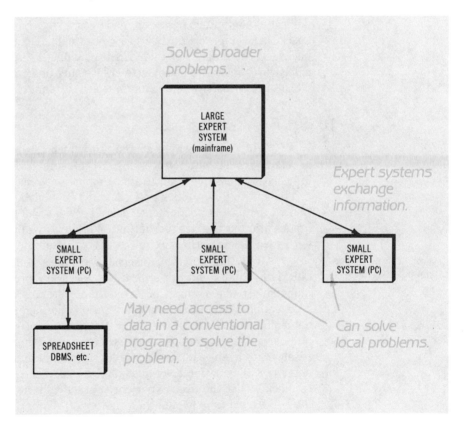

Dedicated Systems

Another type of expert system is one that is buried within a closed or dedicated computer. Like a stand-alone system, it uses one computer to solve one problem. Military weapons computers and factory process-control computers are examples of dedicated systems. Microcomputers are also built into appliances, test instruments, and other equipment. These computers perform no function other than that for which they were intended. Many are hard-wired into the system and cannot be changed or accessed.

Expert systems make dedicated computers more powerful and useful.

While most dedicated computers run standard algorithmic software, more and more are taking advantage of expert systems and other AI programs. By bringing knowledge to bear upon a problem, significant improvements in performance can be achieved. In the future, many of those microprocessors buried in other equipment will be running expert systems as well as standard algorithmic software.

The task of using expert systems and other forms of AI in dedicated computers has been made easier by the introduction of special AI computer hardware. For example, Texas Instruments has packaged the essence of their LISP machine AI workstation into a chip, which makes it possible to create tiny dedicated systems which use AI software written in the LISP language.

Real-Time Systems

The oldest form of computing, which carries on even today, is referred to as batch processing. Here users save up their input information and give it all to the computer at once so that programs can be run to update files and generate new outputs as required. In this way, there is a significant delay between the availability of the input data and the desired output. While many applications can deal with such delays, others require nearly instantaneous computing.

Real-time expert systems solve problems almost as they occur.

Real-time software programs are designed to respond quickly to inputs and to perform the necessary processing almost immediately. An example of a real-time system is an airline reservation system that enables a reservation agent to immediately determine the status of the flight, the number of seats available, the number and type of applicable discounts, and other information. The reservation agent can then make a reservation and immediately enter the information to update the system. The processing is done so quickly that the user experiences practically no delay.

A real-time system in a fighter or bomber aircraft can help a busy pilot make decisions. The expert system might monitor the radar, infrared sensors, and other inputs to reach a conclusion about conditions and recommend a course of action. Since a pilot needs to know "right now," real-time processing is required.

Another real-time example is the computing that goes on in a complex control system. A dedicated computer controlling a chemical plant, for example, typically requires real-time operation.

The computer may sense various conditions such as temperature, flow rates, pressure, and so on. These signals are used by the computer to determine how the control program should be modified. Modifications, in turn, lead to the generation of new control signals. For example, if the temperature is too high, the sensor picks up that fact and the computer produces an output signal that adjusts the temperature to the desired level. In real-time operation, the computer must take the sensor information and process it quickly enough so that the output control signals are generated in a timely and useful manner.

Computer scientists and programmers are just beginning to build real-time expert systems. Because expert systems are large and often slow to execute, they have not been suitable for real-time applications. However, their value is great in many real-time applications and research is underway to make such programs practical.

Very high processing speed is the key to creating useful real-time expert systems.

The key to making a real-time expert system is having a large enough and fast enough computer. In order for the response to be nearly instantaneous, very high processing speed is normally required. The need for processing speed can be reduced somewhat, though, by special software design. There are efficient ways to represent knowledge and do searches that greatly speed up the AI knowledge processing.

As you might expect, an expert system could embody the features of two or more of these types. Embedded and linked systems may be combined. A dedicated system may also feature real-time operation.

HOW EXPERT SYSTEMS ARE USED

Expert systems are only good at solving certain types of problems, but they can be used in a wide range of applications.

Approaching Problem-Solving

Analysis and synthesis are kinds of problem-solving.

People solve problems in one of two basic ways. They either analyze, using inductive reasoning, or they synthesize, using deductive reasoning.

Analysis by Inductive Reasoning

Inductive reasoning is from the specific to the general.

With analysis, you break a large problem down into smaller problems to make the job easier. Or, you start with a solution or goal, then try to accumulate facts that support and prove it. In inductive reasoning, you attempt to reach a general conclusion by examining specific facts or premises; you reason from the specific to the general. Some examples of induction are:

- Diagnosis—Identifying problems or troubles
- Prediction—Foretelling outcomes based on knowledge
- Testing—Searching for items that meet specific criteria
- Classification—Putting items into specific categories

As we will see, these are all excellent jobs for expert systems.

Synthesis by Deductive Reasoning

Deductive reasoning is from the general to the specific.

In synthesis, you work with facts and attempt to build up to a solution or reach a goal. In deductive reasoning, you use broad premises to draw a particular conclusion. That is reasoning from the general to the specific. Some problems requiring synthesis are:

- Design—Creating something new and original from facts, theories, and so on
- Planning—Developing a scheme of steps and their sequence to reach a specific goal
- Configuration—Selecting and assembling individual parts into a useful whole

Again, all of these jobs can be done by expert systems.

Classes of Expert Systems

Now let's examine some of the specific categories of expert systems. Each type requires either analysis or synthesis.

Analyzing and Interpreting Systems

Expert systems help humans deal with an overload of data.

Expert systems are very good at analyzing a large amount of information, interpreting it, and providing an output explanation or recommendation. When huge amounts of information are involved in a problem, it is difficult for a human to remember and keep track of it all. Too much data puts a person into overload. The expert system, however, has no problem dealing with this. Consequently, expert systems can provide a more thorough analysis and interpretation than a human, often providing a better recommendation or more thorough understanding of the situation.

Expert systems that perform interpretation work from input data supplied from a keyboard, or by another computer program, or derived from electronic monitoring sensors. Once the information is available to the system, the inference program uses the input data along with a knowledge base in an attempt to understand the data. It then provides an explanation or draws conclusions from the data.

An example of an analysis/interpretation system is one that does financial planning. It receives as input all of the financial data about a client plus his or her financial goals. The system analyzes all of the data-matching resources and investment opportunities available. The possible investment options are normally very large, and it is difficult, not to mention time-consuming, for a person to figure out a desirable course of action. Today, most financial planning organizations use computers and expert systems to help their clients make good decisions.

Predicting Systems

Expert systems can make intelligent predictions.

Expert systems are good at predicting future results. By using input data about a given situation, a prediction expert system can infer future consequences or outcomes based on knowledge it has. Prediction systems are good at determining likely consequences of given conditions. The knowledge base often contains trend data and historical information as well as cyclical patterns that are applicable. By applying these to the input data, likely outcomes can be reliably predicted. Weather forecasting and stock market directions are good examples of prediction systems.

PROSPECTOR is an example of a prediction system. PROSPECTOR is designed to help geologists locate ore deposits. It contains rules about ore environments and conditions a well as data on rocks and minerals. When it is given geological field survey data, it can predict the likelihood of various types of ores being present at the survey sight. PROSPECTOR has been unusually successful in locating several large, valuable deposits.

Diagnosing and Debugging Systems

Let an expert system figure out what's wrong and suggest corrective action.

Another superior application for expert systems is diagnosing and debugging. Both of these techniques are used in the troubleshooting and repair of equipment. These techniques are also widely used in diagnostic medicine.

A diagnostic expert system is given input data about the behavior of the device, system, or individual. In fact, most expert systems ask a series of questions in an effort to accumulate the input necessary to draw a conclusion. This input data takes the form of symptoms, physical characteristics, recorded performance, and any irregularities or undesired functions. With this information, the inference program scans the knowledge base to determine what is wrong.

While some expert systems perform only diagnosis, others also include debugging characteristics, which means they recommend suitable actions to correct the problems and deficiencies discovered.

One of the broadest uses of expert systems is in the diagnosis and debugging of complex systems. Large computer systems and complex military electronic equipment are good examples of systems that are ideal for expert system use. It is extremely tough for an individual to locate problems in such large and complex systems, but with the help of an expert system, troubles can be located faster and repaired sooner.

One such system is Automated Cable Expertise (ACE), developed at Bell Labs in New Jersey. Used to help find defects in a telephone network, it examines maintenance reports and repair data, determines the location of cable faults, and suggests maintenance procedures.

There are many medical expert systems, each specializing in a specific disease or malady, that can help doctors quickly diagnose and treat patients. An example is PUFF, a system that helps doctors diagnose lung disease. Patient history and special test data are entered and PUFF outputs a decision about possible pulmonary problems and their treatment.

Monitoring and Control Systems

Intelligent control based on feedback can improve the performance of plants, factories, weapons and other systems.

Computers are often used to monitor a process and then provide an output control in response. The computers that control automated factories and chemical plants are examples. Another good application for an expert system is the monitoring and control of a nuclear power plant.

Monitoring is basically the process of observing inputs derived from sensors. A wide variety of sensors can be used to convert physical changes into electrical signals that can be used by a computer. A program is set up to determine whether the monitored signals are within a desired range. In an expert system, the knowledge base contains rules about what to do if the inputs are out of acceptable range. Should any of the sensors indicate an out-of-range condition, the control portion of the computer program is called upon to adjust selected portions of the system in order to bring the sensor data back into the correct range.

This process of monitoring and controlling most often uses feedback, sensory information from the system being controlled. It tells the computer what is happening. The computer continues to control the system until it receives information that the system is going astray or reaching some desired conclusion. Called closed-loop control systems, these systems permit full automation of some process. Such a system is shown in *Figure 2-3*. The outputs from the computer control the system while the sensors determine the status of the system. In between, the computer performs the necessary operations to keep the system on track. Most closed-loop control systems use algorithms for performing the control. Expert systems can be used, however, when an algorithmic solution either isn't available or doesn't fit the type of control problem.

**Figure 2-3.
Closed-Loop Control
System**

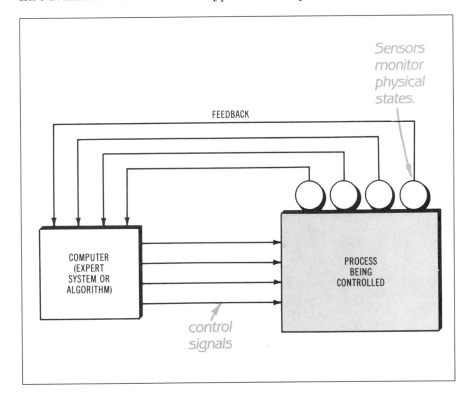

There are few real systems in this field yet, but a demonstration prototype called FALCON has been created to test the concept. FALCON monitors sensors, gauges, and other inputs from a chemical processing plant. It analyzes the data and tries to identify causes of problems in the process which can then be corrected by plant operators. Full closed-loop control is not yet available.

Design Systems

Design is the process of creating a product, device, or procedure. Given a set of specifications, requirements, and constraints, the designer creates or develops the desired object or procedure.

Expert system-based CAD programs free the engineer or designer for more creative tasks.

Design requires a tremendous amount of knowledge, much of which can be contained within an expert system to assist a designer in creating the product or process. Today, there are computer-aided design (CAD) systems to help engineers design electronic circuits, integrated circuits, printed circuit boards, mechanical components, and architectural structures. Automobile manufacturers use CAD techniques in creating new car designs. Some examples of prototype design systems are PEACE and SADD, both of which accept as inputs the description and specification of an electronic circuit. The output is a synthesized circuit that is simulated to test its validity and performance.

While design is essentially a creative process, much of it entails the application of standard rules and procedures. An expert system is good at providing this part of the design. As with most expert systems, the goal is not to replace the designer but to assist him or her in completing the design competently and within time and cost constraints.

Planning Systems

Expert systems help humans quickly create plans for complex operations.

When a goal is acknowledged, all of the actions required to achieve it can be identified. Then these actions can be properly sequenced to achieve the desired goal. Planning is the process of putting the steps in sequence.

Very large plans are extremely difficult to construct. Humans are generally good at planning because they can accommodate a considerable amount of input data and they possess knowledge that they can bring to bear in creating the plan. But the greater the number of people, actions, resources, and outcomes involved, the more difficult creating the plan becomes. Today, computers are being widely used to help develop plans. Such plans may cover the management of a large-scale development project or the planning of a factory's manufacturing sequence for optimum output. Another example is the planning of military strategy and tactics.

A number of planning expert systems have been developed. IMACS is used to help plan manufacturing capacity and manage inventory. ISIS helps plan factory job schedules. PTRANS helps create a plan for manufacturing custom configurations of complex computer systems. While these systems are all used in manufacturing, the principles could be applied to any field.

Instructional Systems

Expert systems can be used as intelligent automated tutors to improve instruction.

As we saw earlier, an expert system can be used to teach by imparting the knowledge that is at the core of the system.

Many computer-based training (CBT) or computer-assisted instruction (CAI) programs are available to teach specific subjects. But such programs have a fixed content and sequence that is not best for every student's learning style. An expert system can solve that problem.

To do this, an expert system is used to evaluate a student's level of knowledge and understanding. With this information, it can adjust the instructional process to the student's needs.

Because they are extremely difficult to construct, expert systems have not been widely developed for instructional purposes. The few research systems that have been built, however, have proven remarkably successful, and it is to be expected that instructional expert systems will be more widely available when faster, easier ways are discovered to build them.

SOPHIE is a research prototype of an instructional system. It was designed to teach technicians how to troubleshoot and repair electronic circuits. SOPHIE simulates circuit operation and allows faults to be introduced so that circuit action can be analyzed. Measurements can be taken so that the problem can be diagnosed. Initial testing of such systems are encouraging because they offer a new, perhaps improved, way of teaching.

The Human Factor

Even though expert systems mimic human thought processes, they are not intended to replace you. Expert systems are a tool to help you do your job faster, easier, and more competently. They can increase your capabilities by giving you extensive knowledge that you can bring to bear on problems; with their use, you can improve your productivity.

An expert system is just a tool. It's up to the user to make the final decision.

But you are still in control. The expert system may give you an answer, conclusion, or recommendation, but the final decision is up to you. If you don't believe or trust the output, ignore it and draw your own conclusions. Use your own judgement as to when to apply an expert system's output.

WHAT EXPERT SYSTEMS ARE NOT

Just because a program solves a problem or makes a decision doesn't mean that it is an expert system.

Whether a program is an expert system often isn't germane to the user. The user cannot tell whether heuristic symbolic processing is going on or whether an algorithm is being solved. For this reason, expert systems are sometimes confused with other types of software that appear to perform similar functions, including data base management systems, decision software, and decision support systems (DSS). All of these use conventional algorithmic approaches to problem-solving even though the kinds of problems solved may be similar to those solved by expert systems.

Data Base Management Systems (DBMS)

A DBMS is a collection of related facts stored in a computer for fast, convenient retrieval.

A data base management system is a software package that allows a user to create and manage large files of data, called a "data base." A data base is sometimes confused with a knowledge base. A data base comprises small units of data called records, which comprise individual data elements called fields. For example, in a customer record, the name, address, city, state, zip code, and telephone number may each represent a field. A record in an inventory file may have fields representing part name and number, source, quantity on hand, and cost. *Figure 2-4* shows the basic structure of a DBMS.

While a record is a unit of data containing facts and figures rather than knowledge, a knowledge base comprises individual "chunks" of knowledge. A common form of expressing knowledge is called a "rule." A typical rule might be "*If* the regulator output voltage is zero *and* the input to the regulator is normal *then* the regulator is defective."

You can readily see the difference between an element of data and an element of knowledge. We'll examine rules in Chapter 3.

Figure 2-4.
An Inventory Data Base

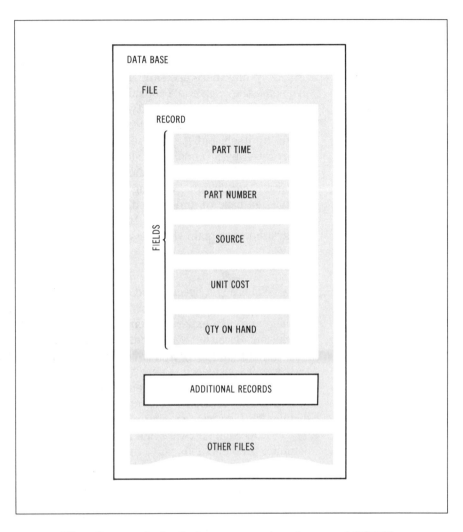

The other confusion between expert systems and DBMS arises from the way they are manipulated. The knowledge base or the data base is searched. Search and pattern-matching techniques are used to locate individual data items and to identify common fields in a DBMS; similar techniques are used in expert systems to identify conditions in a knowledge base. But while the goal of the search in the DBMS is only to locate specific items, often with some common element, the search of a knowledge base is conducted in order to link units of knowledge in an effort to form a logical chain of inferences duplicating human reasoning. The output of a DBMS search is typically a listing of records and files with a common key

A DBMS is not an expert system and vice versa.

or field. These are usually output for further analysis. The output of the expert system is an answer or conclusion drawn by applying the knowledge in the knowledge base to the problem.

While there are similarities between the two, the kinds of problems they solve are considerably different. DBMS and other types of file-management software are used primarily to store great volumes of information and access them readily. The data may be useful by itself, but it must be understood, analyzed, and interpreted by a human in order for it to be of value.

On the other hand, the expert system provides some kind of an output conclusion. Working with input data, it uses the knowledge base to understand the problem sufficiently to make a recommendation or decision. It may even provide an explanation subsystem to explain the decision.

Decision Software

Mathematical techniques can be used to help make tough decisions.

There is a special kind of algorithmic software designed to help individuals make decisions. These programs examine data given to them and, like expert systems, suggest an optimum decision or conclusion. Because they do not use symbolic representation or use search and pattern matching as their basic method of manipulation, they aren't considered expert systems or AI programs. Such decision-making programs are implemented with a number of widely known mathematical decision algorithms and, in use, you cannot easily distinguish a decision-making program from an expert system.

Decision software can help you make a decision on a complex problem. Typically, the goal is to choose the best of several different alternatives. The criteria for selecting a particular outcome are defined in numerical terms. Their importance or priority is weighted, and by converting the criteria into numerical values, mathematical algorithms can be used to process them and select the most desirable outcome. Decision software provides a precise solution, whereas an expert system may offer only an approximate solution, or a guess, or no solution at all.

Decision Support Systems (DSS)

DSS helps managers run large, complex organizations by providing ways to analyze data, understand it, and make decisions.

A decision support system (DSS) is a collection of programs used for decision-making. Such programs help management in forecasting, planning, and managing large enterprises. Decision support systems usually incorporate some kind of decision software.

Many DSS also include a modeling capability that enables a mathematical simulation of a situation to be built in order to test various tactics and strategies. The model is usually a mathematical realization of a financial or other situation that can be reduced to numbers and calculations. Once a model of the system has been built, various approaches can be tested. The input data can be manipulated and the various outcomes determined. Modeling permits real-world actions to be tested so that the best decision can be made.

Decision support systems use conventional procedural data processing to achieve their results; they shouldn't be confused with expert systems.

CHOOSING THE BEST SOFTWARE

The approach used to solve a problem is relatively unimportant as long as a good solution or decision is reached. The usefulness of any software, be it algorithmic or symbolic, is based upon its value to its user. Neither AI nor algorithmic problem-solving is superior. The best kind of program to use depends upon the problem; if it does the job, the approach is irrelevant.

Expert systems are greatly enhancing the performance of DBMS, decision programs, and DSS. For example, expert systems are being combined with DBMS to further improve their ability to find the correct data and format it properly. Decision support systems are also incorporating expert systems, providing users with the information and knowledge they need to make good decisions.

What Have We Learned?

1. There are five main types of expert systems: stand-alone, hybrid, linked, dedicated, and real time.

2. An algorithmic program may be embedded in an expert system or vice versa to form an integrated or hybrid program.

3. The best performance is usually obtained with a mix of AI and conventional software.

4. Linked expert systems combine multiple expert systems or provide access to conventional software such as spreadsheets and DBMS.

5. A dedicated expert system usually runs on a microprocessor buried deep in a weapon, instrument, or controller. It solves one problem only.

6. Real-time expert systems execute so quickly that response from input through processing to output seems instantaneous.

7. The two main approaches to problem-solving are analysis and synthesis.

8. Inductive reasoning is drawing a general conclusion from the specific facts. It is analogous to analysis.

9. Deductive reasoning is the examination of general facts to reach a specific conclusion. It is analogous to synthesis.

10. Expert systems are good at solving problems of induction such as diagnosis, prediction, testing, and classification.

11. Expert systems can readily solve problems requiring deductive methods such as design, configuration, and planning.

12. Expert systems can serve an intelligent function in closed-loop control systems.

13. Expert systems are an excellent instructional tool.

14. A user may choose to ignore the advice of an expert system in making a decision. Expert systems are only electronic consultants; the user has control over the final solution and its application.

15. Expert systems are sometimes confused with algorithmic programs that also make decisions or solve similar problems. Some of the programs are data base management systems, decision software, and decision support systems.

Quiz for Chapter 2

1. An expert system with a built-in algorithmic program is called a(n):
   a. linked program.
   b. dedicated program.
   c. hybrid program.
   d. stand-alone program.

2. Dedicated expert systems usually run on a:
   a. buried microprocessor.
   b. personal computer.
   c. minicomputer.
   d. mainframe computer.

3. True or false: expert systems may reference conventional programs such as spreadsheets and DBMS.

4. Expert systems that execute without apparent delay are called:
   a. fast.
   b. dedicated.
   c. instantaneous.
   d. real time.

5. The two main methods of problem-solving are:
   a. thinking and guessing.
   b. analysis and synthesis.
   c. general and specific.
   d. forward and backward.

6. Using general premises to reach a specific conclusion is called:
   a. forward thinking.
   b. deductive reasoning.
   c. backward thinking.
   d. inductive reasoning.

7. When you use induction, you reason from:
   a. specific to general.
   b. front to back.
   c. back to front.
   d. general to particular.

8. Breaking a complex problem down into simpler parts is called:
   a. synthesis.
   b. hypothesis.
   c. dissection.
   d. analysis.

9. Which of the following is *not* a good task for an expert system?
   a. Designing.
   b. Planning.
   c. Calculating.
   d. Configuring.

10. Which of the following is *not* a good application for an expert system?
    a. Classification.
    b. Diagnosis.
    c. Prediction.
    d. Translation.

11. A data base management system is made up of a collection of:
    a. rules.
    b. frames.
    c. files.
    d. fields.

12. Software that includes programs for simulation and decision-making for management is referred to as a(n):
    a. decision program.
    b. decision support system.
    c. expert system.
    d. DBMS.

13. An operation common to both DBMS and expert systems is:
    a. calculation.
    b. rule-matching.
    c. sorting.
    d. searching.

14. True or false: AI software is superior to algorithmic software in making decisions.

15. Expert systems are superior for helping humans deal with:
    a. excessive information.
    b. lack of data.
    c. complex mathematical operations.
    d. gut reactions.

16. What kind of expert system would help locate problems in a complex system?
    a. Prediction.
    b. Diagnosis.
    c. Planning.
    d. Interpretation.

17. An expert system to help create new products is good at:
    a. prediction.
    b. interpretation.
    c. troubleshooting.
    d. design.

18. The name of an expert system that uses feedback is:
    a. monitor and control.
    b. design.
    c. planning.
    d. instruction.

19. An expert system that helps organize actions and resources to achieve a goal is used in:
    a. planning.
    b. design.
    c. configuration.
    d. analysis.

20. A key factor in the use of an expert system is that:
    a. it is a direct replacement of a human.
    b. computers are better than humans at problem-solving.
    c. the user has the final say in the decision.
    d. even ignorant humans can solve complex problems.

Applications of Expert Systems

ABOUT THIS CHAPTER

In Chapter 2 we surveyed the major applications areas for expert systems. Most real-world expert systems fall into one of two basic categories. We begin this chapter with a look at these major classes. The remainder of the chapter is a detailed discussion of practical expert systems used by business, industry, government, and military.

Trying to specify applications categories for expert systems is somewhat akin to attempting to specify all of the ways computers can be used. Although the application is incredibly broad, certain types of problems yield best to an expert system solution. When you complete this chapter, you will have a pretty good feel for how expert systems are being used currently and whether or not an expert system may be of value to you.

CONSULTATION SYSTEMS

We mentioned earlier that expert systems are sometimes called knowledge-based systems. We didn't distinguish between them because, in general, they both rely on built-in knowledge to advise users. Some developers, however, do make this distinction between expert and knowledge-based programs: expert systems contain the heuristics of one or more experts while knowledge-based systems contain mostly knowledge, facts, and information not necessarily derived from experience or problem-solving practice. Some programs may actually contain a mix.

Both expert and knowledge-based systems primarily serve as smart consultants to their users. As a result, they are also called "consultation" systems.

Most consultation systems do one of the following:

Most consultation systems perform troubleshooting and select among alternatives.

- Perform troubleshooting—Diagnose problems, observe symptoms, and look for their cause. Troubleshooting can apply to humans with illnesses or complex systems with faults.

- Select best alternative—Provide a wide range of answer choices typically known to most users in advance. The expert system attempts to satisfy the constraints set by the inputs in selecting the best solution.

As you read about the specific applications in the sections to follow, keep these broad areas in mind and attempt to match them to the problems described.

Most of the expert systems under development or available today are used in one or more of these fields: finance, engineering and scientific, manufacturing, computing, government, and military. In the following sections, we want to take an in-depth look at each of these areas.

FINANCIAL EXPERT SYSTEMS

There may be more expert systems to solve financial problems than any other type.

Almost every business today uses a computer to perform its basic accounting functions, such as general ledger, accounts receivable, accounts payable, and payroll. Further, financial institutions such as banks rely heavily upon computers to keep track of accounts, loans, investments, and other financial dealings. Insurance companies—in reality, a major type of financial institution —rely almost exclusively on computers to keep track of their customers, claims, and investments.

With these applications already in use, you wouldn't imagine that there could be much new in the use of computers in the financial arena. Yet, the financial field is one of the largest if not the largest arena for expert system application.

Much of financial computation has to do with simple number-crunching. This involves storing financial information and then performing transactions on it as conditions change. This kind of computation is perfect for computers because it permits simple algorithms to do most of the computing. Such computations are performed on raw financial data to produce new financial data. The computer also provides a convenient way to store and retrieve all that data. This saves a lot of time and effort, but the computer doesn't replace the human expert in analyzing and using the financial information; the financial data and reports generated by computers are only valuable when they are understood.

It takes a financial expert to analyze and apply the financial information available, and this is where expert systems come in. With expert systems, computers can analyze financial data and provide answers to questions, solutions to problems, or recommendations for decisions. Humans, who can be overloaded by excessive financial information and find it difficult to work their way through tons of data, can program financial expertise into the computer, allowing the computer to work with the most complex information and make sense of it.

The Banking Field

Banks are beginning to develop and use expert systems. For example, banks have discovered that expert systems are excellent for credit evaluation. Most banks have standard criteria for evaluating loan applications. This information is collected by a loan officer, who evaluates the inputs and, based on knowledge of the potential borrower and the bank's standards and risk limits, decides whether to grant the loan. This knowledge can also be put into an expert system so that a decision on a loan can be made easily by someone other than a bank officer. By building an expert system to perform credit evaluation, banks can make more consistent lending decisions. While such expert systems will not replace loan officers, it can help them make faster and better loan decisions. And it can enable the bank to use other, less experienced employees to make loan decisions.

Another area in which banks are beginning to consider the use of expert systems is investment and money management strategies. Banks must be constantly aware of ongoing financial changes in order to make good investment decisions. It has been estimated that commercial banks move from 10 to 20 percent of their total assets daily. This requires close monitoring of the financial world and making intelligent investment decisions daily. The stock market and interest rates also change daily. An expert system that can provide general guidance for making good financial decisions would be welcomed by most banks. Many banks are working on just such a system. Once available, it will help bank officials develop better strategies and implement them quickly.

Taxes

Expert systems that help individuals and companies make good tax decisions are now available. Managing taxes is a vital part of the financial strategies of both individuals and companies. As complex as the tax code is, it takes an expert to suggest the best tax strategies. This kind of knowledge is relatively easy to program into an expert system.

The Big Eight accounting firms as well as other tax advisory organizations are building and testing expert systems. The expertise of senior tax experts and auditors is being captured in a form that allows others with less experience and knowledge to advise clients of their best tax strategies.

Even the IRS is looking into the use of expert systems. The IRS now uses computers to record and analyze tax returns. While the current analysis programs can only make selected checks on specific deductions, improved analysis of tax returns could be done if expert systems were employed.

The IRS is looking into the development of expert systems that will reduce human involvement in the analysis and processing of tax returns. Such expert systems would provide a more thorough analysis and better pinpoint audit candidates. For example, high on the list of business-related tax returns are expenses for travel and entertainment. The IRS scrutinizes such expenses for violations. An appropriate expert system would eliminate the present random brute-force technique, which leads to many unnecessary audits while letting many violators escape attention.

Stocks and Bonds

Performance in the financial markets will be improved by smart consultation systems.

Expert systems are being developed to help stock brokers and traders recommend and sell stocks and bonds. Expert systems can help analyze companies, markets, and the economy by applying general knowledge and heuristics. This can help improve the quality of recommendations that stock brokers make to clients.

An expert system can also help improve the pricing of stocks and bonds. For example, trends could be anticipated by observing the signals that typically presage price changes. By programming trading history and market conditions into an expert system, stocks and options traders can adjust their trading strategies, predict price moves, and otherwise make better decisions.

Financial Planning

Numerous financial planning expert systems are available to reduce a mass of data into a workable plan.

Expert systems can be of great help in financial planning. Financial planning entails analysis of the financial situation of an individual or a company and involves a variety of considerations, including taxes, investments, insurance, and, in the case of individuals, estate planning. Knowing their financial goals, the expert system can formulate specific plans to achieve those goals within the constraints of their financial resources and external conditions.

Numerous expert systems are available to help financial planners. Typically, the financial planner must analyze a considerable amount of information provided by the client. The financial planner also must factor in new tax laws, interest rates, inflation, and investment opportunities in order to assemble a plan that suits the client's needs. It is extremely difficult to analyze and retain all of this information. It is a classic case of the human overload condition. An expert system, however, can be programmed with all of this information, and it can analyze a financial situation quickly and recommend a suitable plan.

Financial planning expert systems combine the knowledge of financial planners, tax experts, insurance experts, estate planners, and economists, among others. The output of such an expert system is a financial plan that will advise clients on what investments to make and how to better utilize their capital in order to reach their objectives.

Business Financial Management

Business management expert systems can be used alone or as a supplement to decision support systems to help management make the best decisions.

Expert systems are being developed to help executives better manage their companies. These expert systems perform a variety of financial analyses and make recommendations to management.

A business's financial condition is evaluated by considering such standard business documents as income statements and balance sheets. Using these documents, an expert system can perform a cash flow analysis, for example. Based on the results of that analysis, the expert system can make recommendations for improving cash flow. For example, it may suggest that the accounting methods used in dealing with company inventory be reconsidered.

Other business expert systems are used to evaluate business plans. A plan for a new company, product, or market can be analyzed, potential problems identified, and recommendations for improvement made. Such expert systems can also help with capital planning and with mergers and acquisitions. A good expert system of this type can even include subjective factors that an algorithmic program could not deal with. Such expert systems could factor in heuristics about the status of an industry, customer opinions, things that worked and didn't work in the past, and other "fuzzy" factors.

The Insurance Field

The insurance industry is just now beginning to use expert systems. The largest current use is in underwriting. An underwriting expert system advisor helps an individual calculate the risk involved in taking on a particular insurance policy. To analyze all the factors involved in providing insurance is a difficult and time-consuming job. Experts with a lot of experience do the job best, but often there is just too much work for them to do. An underwriting expert system lets a less experienced individual make the same judgements. Such expert systems save time and money and at the same time improve decision-making, leading to lower risk.

Another expert system used in the insurance industry helps check insurance forms to be sure they have been completed by the customer properly. The forms are long and complex, and often their use and value is not explained to the applicant. The form is often useless without the correct data. The expert system examines the form to determine if complete information has been provided.

SCIENCE AND ENGINEERING EXPERT SYSTEMS

For years, computers have aided the technical community's research and development efforts by solving tough math problems, analyzing data accumulated in tests and experiments, and verifying new designs through simulation.

Now expert systems are giving technical workers even more computer power. Engineers are using knowledge-based computer-aided design (CAD) systems to create new products. Doctors are using expert systems to diagnose and treat illnesses. Engineers and technicians are creating expert systems that help them diagnose problems in complex systems. The number of potential applications is enormous. We're going to take a look at some of the more popular ones in use.

Repair/Maintenance Expert Systems

A major category of expert system is technical equipment diagnostics. These systems are designed to help individuals troubleshoot and repair complex systems. Provided with a set of symptoms and observations, the system can logically reason through the problem and suggest possible causes and solutions.

Like most other expert systems, troubleshooting expert systems improve productivity and save time and money. They enable a technician or field service engineer to diagnose the problem and make the repair faster, putting defective equipment back to work sooner. Not only work and money is lost when expensive systems are down. In some cases, the consequences of inoperable equipment are very serious; defense and medical systems are examples.

Since troubleshooting expert systems are difficult and expensive to develop, most of them are used on large, complex, and expensive equipment or where large volumes of the equipment must be serviced. Examples of these are large computer and telephone systems, and data communications networks. The military also uses expert systems to help correct faults inside major weapons systems. For example, the Navy uses expert systems to help locate troubles in radar systems. The larger and more complex the system, the more suitable it is for troubleshooting by an expert system.

Auto manufacturers are discovering that diagnostic expert systems can greatly facilitate both the manufacturing and servicing of automobiles. For example, Ford uses an expert system to help diagnose machine tool problems and problems on manufacturing tools such as robots. When such a machine or tool malfunctions, it can halt production. Rapid troubleshooting and repair is important. An expert system can help keep the production lines rolling.

General Motors is using expert systems to help diagnose and repair electrical systems and the on-board computers now used in most new cars. These systems are complex and spotting problems is difficult. An expert system simplifies and speeds up the process. Many of these expert systems run on a computer that is connected to the car's electrical system. This enables the computer to read signals from the car's computer in order to determine its status.

Many computer manufacturers use diagnostic expert systems in both manufacturing and field service applications. IBM uses a diagnostic expert system to help locate faults in disk drives during the final manufacturing stages. With the use of the expert system, technicians can repair these defective units quickly with a minimum waste of replacement parts.

Computer companies are using expert systems to help clone their top field service engineers. Many computer users simply cannot deal with the problems that a defective computer creates. When an important computer goes down, day or night, one of the few company experts may be called upon to diagnose the problem and get the system running again. As usual, though, top troubleshooting experts are spread thin and often are unavailable even during a crisis. With an expert system, the faults can be quickly diagnosed and repaired by others.

General Electric Corporation designed and built one of the first knowledge-based troubleshooting systems. The system was designed to improve the maintenance of diesel-electric locomotives. Only a few individuals in the company had the experience to troubleshoot such large and complex machines. The GE expert system codified the troubleshooting experience of those few.

General Electric also developed an expert system for helping to maintain and repair jet aircraft engines. Such systems let less-skilled mechanics diagnose engine problems and make repairs that otherwise would have to be done by senior personnel.

Many additional expert systems are in use or being developed to troubleshoot complex systems. These include such major installations as chemical plants and nuclear power plants. These systems often use many sensors to assess conditions within the system and to provide continuous inputs to the diagnostic software. With the latest information available, the expert system can make an accurate estimate of conditions and pinpoint faults and corrective action.

With the scarcity of human troubleshooting experts and the high cost of downtime for sophisticated equipment, we can expect that many expert systems will be developed. While such systems cannot replace field service engineers and repair technicians, they will improve the technicians' productivity and increase their effectiveness. Both the customer and the servicing organization benefit.

Medical Expert Systems

Doctors use expert systems to speed up diagnosis, confirm their own diagnosis, or to provide advice on certain diseases.

The medical field may make more use of expert systems than any other field. Dozens of advisory programs have been developed to help physicians diagnose a particular illness and, in some cases, to prescribe treatment.

The oldest medical expert system is MYCIN which we described in Chapter 1 as one of the pioneer expert systems. Many systems have spun off MYCIN and the work itself encouraged others to create similar systems. *Table 3-1* summarizes some of the medical expert systems available today.

One of the more ambitious undertakings in the medical field is the development of an expert system that mimics the capabilities of an internist. Such a system is CADUCEUS, which was developed and has been extensively tested by the University of Pittsburgh School of Medicine. It can diagnose the hundreds of maladies composing the broad field of internal medicine which encompasses most adult illnesses.

Table 3-1.
Medical Expert Systems

System	Purpose
ONCOCIN	Assists physicians in treating cancer patients with chemotherapy by selecting the appropriate treatment based on the patient's diagnosis and previous treatment
PUFF	Helps identify lung disorders
CASNET/GLAUCOMA	Helps diagnose glaucoma and other eye diseases and prescribe treatment
GUIDON	Instructional system to teach how to select antimicrobial therapy for bacterial infections
Drug Interaction Critic	Advisory system that helps doctors prescribe drugs when other drugs are being used

Prior to using CADUCEUS, the doctor takes the patient history and does the normal exploratory work, including a thorough medical examination. This information, along with basic laboratory data, is entered into the computer and is used as a starting point for diagnosis.

Given enough data, the system usually provides an accurate diagnosis almost immediately. Even if insufficient data is available, CADUCEUS may produce possible diagnoses. At this point, the program begins to ask questions to collect more detailed data. Additional tests and measurements may be required. With this information, the program quickly narrows the possibilities and provides a firm diagnosis.

The principal benefit of medical expert systems is that they can help doctors quickly diagnose complex illnesses. Because there are so many distinct diseases, it's difficult for a physician to keep track of them all. Again, expert systems are excellent at assisting individuals in an overload condition. Another benefit is that expert systems also enable a doctor to confirm a hunch or to explore alternative diagnoses in a difficult case.

Most medical expert systems have a competency just about on par with a good human physician. In fact, CADUCEUS has actually passed the certifying exam for the Board of Internal Medicine. While medical expert systems are remarkably reliable, they can make errors, so the doctor always remains fully in control. The advice of the computer may be helpful, but the physician makes the final judgement.

A program similar to CADUCEUS, also created at the University of Pittsburgh, is the *Electronic Textbook of Medicine*. It contains information on more than seven hundred diseases. Its knowledge base is an accumulation of the contents of textbooks, journals, and interviews with specialists. Such a "textbook" permits rapid access to a massive amount of medical knowledge. The system can be questioned to ask for all its knowledge about a particular disease, or it can be used as an expert system for diagnosis based on symptoms and test results.

Another major medical expert system, HELP, is designed to assist a physician in determining which drug and dosage to administer. Given sufficient input, HELP will quickly zero in on the right drug from among the thousands available. The system is unusually good at prescribing obscure drugs for unusual illnesses that may not be familiar to the physician. The HELP expert system is a money-saver; it enables the physician to avoid having to experiment with a number of different drugs before finding the correct one.

While there may be more expert systems for the medical field than for any other field, few doctors are using them yet. The reason for this is that most expert systems are closely held research prototypes. Few, if any, doctors outside the developers get to use such systems. As a result, no commercial medical systems are widely distributed. This problem is pervasive in expert system development.

Some doctors refuse to use expert systems, calling them the "cookbook" approach to medicine. Despite the fact that the physician is always in control, the Federal Drug Administration is considering regulations that would require medical expert systems to be FDA-approved prior to their use. Such regulations, while well-meaning to protect the consumer, threaten creative research and development. FDA approvals typically take many years to achieve and the red tape involved could seriously curtail worthwhile development efforts.

Engineering Expert Systems

Engineers can be more productive when they use knowledge-based CAD systems.

Although computers have been used in design for over twenty years, a high percentage of engineers haven't tried the technology. Continuing development has lowered computer costs and given computers the graphic power to be effective design tools. Expert systems now provide a way to preserve and package design skill and experience, enabling engineers to increase their productivity.

Such CAD systems have found wide application in electronics. Engineers use expert systems to help them lay out printed circuit boards, design complex digital logic circuits, and configure integrated circuits.

Most CAD programs are algorithmic in nature. They perform calculations and analysis and solve for formulas into which the engineer can plug various values. Other design programs are simulations. The computer provides a convenient way to build a mathematical or logical model of an electronic circuit or a mechanical component. This lets the engineer test the design concept prior to investing considerable time and money in building prototypes. Once the computerized design has been verified and proven, the real-world hardware can be built.

Many design duties do not lend themselves to an algorithmic solution or a simulation. They are fuzzier in their objectives and often require the creativity and mental acuity only humans possess. Now artificial intelligence techniques can solve some of those problems. Expert systems, in particular, are being created to package the knowledge of engineers so others can use it to produce superior designs in less time at lower cost.

PCB Layout

Let an expert system take the time and worry out of designing printed circuit boards.

One of the most difficult engineering jobs is the layout of printed circuit boards (PCB). Once an engineer completes an electronic circuit design, all of the components must be located on a circuit board and the copper interconnection patterns designed. In the past, this was done by engineers or technicians and drafters experienced in this work. The entire process is extremely time-consuming and many designs must often be tried to achieve a satisfactory end product.

Computers were engaged in printed circuit board layouts nearly a decade ago. Then the algorithmic methods required large, powerful minicomputers to operate successfully. The high cost of such systems prevented them from being widely used. Today, expert systems as well as algorithmic programs are being used on small engineering workstations and personal computers to perform PCB layout.

By combining production rules with selected algorithms, a board design can be completed very quickly. Most systems complete the job in just a fraction of the time that it takes for an engineer or drafter to complete the job manually. And, not only is the speed of design improved, but its accuracy is also.

As electronic components and circuits grow more complex, the cost of expert system PCB layout programs will be easier to justify. Large complex multilayer boards are incredibly difficult to design, but automated expert system software makes fast work of them. As prices of this software continue to decline, more of them will be used.

Integrated Circuit Design

Arranging and interconnecting the thousands of components on a high-density IC chip is a nightmare that disappears when an expert system is used.

Expert systems are also being used for the design of complex integrated circuits. In many respects, laying out an integrated circuit is similar to creating a printed circuit board. Components must be located in a given space and interconnected with a minimum of cross-overs and extra layers. By providing design rules and layout constraints in the knowledge base, expert systems can be used to solve specific design problems, particularly for very large-scale integrated (VLSI) chips. Complex gate arrays and applications-specific integrated circuits (ASIC) are ideal candidates for design by an expert system. As with printed circuit design, design time and costs are reduced with expert systems. But perhaps more important is that with this type of AI software, humans can actually design such circuits. Without that help, most humans are unable to keep track of all of the details necessary to design a VLSI circuit.

The manufacturers of computer-aided engineering (CAE) workstations are beginning to use rule-based expert systems in their products. These specialized computers run software specifically created to help engineers design digital and analog electronic circuits. Engineers can sit at the workstations and build and test their circuits prior to making them real with hardware. While most of these workstations use algorithmic techniques and simulation, the newer systems have rule-based segments that can be called upon in selected applications. Routine designs of standard circuits are expedited in this way.

Manufacturing Expert Systems

Expert systems help optimize the manufacturing process by maximizing output and quality while reducing time and costs.

Manufacturing is one field in which expert systems really prove their worth. The main goal of manufacturing is to produce a large quantity of high-quality goods in the least time at the lowest cost. In other words, the objective of manufacturing is very high productivity. By bringing knowledge to bear on manufacturing operations, expert systems can significantly improve productivity.

Manufacturing operations typically use less-skilled workers to do the actual manufacturing work. Some experts may be available in the more technical areas, but, because knowledge is not widely represented, productivity and quality often suffer. By packaging critical knowledge into expert systems that workers of any skill can use, significant improvements can be achieved.

The use of expert systems to improve manufacturing begins with the design and setup of production lines capable of producing the greatest output. Those experienced in manufacturing operations can bring their knowledge to bear on this as new plants are built or as improvements are made to established production lines.

In existing manufacturing operations, expert systems can optimize the production process by helping to identify critical parameters in order that they be given proper attention. Expert systems that enable manufacturing engineers to evaluate alternative operations and processes help improve production planning. Such systems can also help manufacturing managers understand and improve on such elements as lead time, materials handling, and inventory control.

Expert systems have great potential in automotive manufacturing. While no major expert systems are in use at this writing, all three major U.S. manufacturers are planning systems or have them under development. Such expert systems should go a long way toward improving output, lowering costs, and increasing quality to help make U.S. manufacturers more competitive with Japanese and European car manufacturers.

Much of the manufacturing process is automated. Computers, numerically controlled machines, and programmable controllers operate the machines that produce parts and materials and assemble them. Many manufacturing operations also use robots. In some cases, the machines and robots replace humans in an effort to speed up production. Where this is true, expert systems can be used to make the controllers smarter and more autonomous. Expert systems combined with sensors in a closed-loop feedback arrangement allow the machines to adjust to their environment, thereby minimizing errors.

While there are few manufacturing expert systems in use today, many are under development. One of the first generic manufacturing expert systems helps manufacturing executives analyze current procedures and plan more efficient operations. The system takes the manufacturer's plant data and, using a production-rule knowledge base, provides advice to the user. The knowledge base contains general information about manufacturing operations and the logic underlying the relationships between the various manufacturing procedures. Applying this knowledge to the user's data, the system then points out flaws in the manufacturing process and, where possible, suggests more efficient methods. Such suggestions might include recommendations of places for expansion and the need for additional machinery. The expert system can help evaluate trade-offs.

Most manufacturing expert systems, however, are more specialized. They focus on a productivity problem specific to the plant and product being manufactured. For example, a number of expert systems have been developed to aid in the assembly of printed circuit boards. One of these systems helps to set up the sequence of hand-assembly steps in a large complex board. It sorts through the design and specification information and presents to the assembly workers a step-by-step procedure on a computer screen. Such an expert system is expected to greatly reduce defect rates and thus increase output quantity and quality simultaneously.

Another manufacturing expert system of this type helps reduce defects in the soldering of printed circuit boards. Today's large complex boards include a variety of semiconductors, both integrated circuit and discrete component devices, as well as other electronic components and various connectors. The soldering parameters for each of these parts are often different. Different parts of the board may have to be soldered separately in order to avoid heat damage. Today, most printed circuit board soldering is done by automatic flow soldering machines. Often these are computer controlled so that the various parameters can be changed continuously during the soldering process. This allows even complex boards to be soldered properly based upon their layout and heat-transfer limitations. The expert system helps inexperienced personnel program the computer to provide the correct operation.

Expert systems are also being used to help in assembling complex technical equipment. One system helps configure and assemble disk drive systems. In general, the assembly process is fairly straightforward, but there are dozens of configurations to be manufactured. An expert system helps sort out the materials requirements for each configuration and provides appropriate assembly instructions. Such expert systems greatly reduce the errors in assembly operations. This increases output productivity, lowers costs, and prevents unnecessary rework and waste of materials.

Another manufacturing expert system is used in welding operations. When a plant must perform welding on a wide variety of materials, the choice of process is often difficult. An expert system has been developed to help recommend types of welding electrodes to use based on the materials to be welded and other key parameters. Welding is a critical manufacturing operation and the integrity of the final product depends upon the quality and stability of the welds. Such a system helps ensure that the correct materials and processes are matched up.

Diagnostic expert systems are also used in manufacturing operations.

A major part of manufacturing operations is testing and troubleshooting. Once the product has been manufactured, it must be tested to ensure that it meets all specifications and operates properly. Should the manufactured product be defective, it is sent to a troubleshooting and repair area to be fixed. As a result, manufacturing operations also use diagnostic expert systems to speed up and improve the troubleshooting and repair of defective units. For example, IBM has a diagnostic expert system that it uses in its disk drive manufacturing plants. This expert system has saved IBM millions of dollars in worker time and waste parts reduction.

In plants that produce chemicals and even foods, expert systems are being called upon to help control the processes and ensure minimum processing plant downtime. For example, Campbell's Soup Company has developed an expert system that helps it troubleshoot and maintain the hydrostatic and rotary sterilizers. Known as cookers, these huge systems are designed to kill botulism bacteria in canned soup. The proper operation of these cookers is essential to turning out the high volume of soups Campbell is known for. The troubleshooting and repair of these cookers is an extremely specialized talent residing with only a few experts. The knowledge of a retiring expert was packaged into an expert system that Campbell's manufacturing managers throughout the world can use to troubleshoot and repair problems in the cookers.

COMPUTER-RELATED APPLICATIONS

Data processing managers and computer programmers are discovering ways that expert systems can solve some of their computer-related problems. As a result, there is growing use of expert systems in companies with large data processing (DP) and management information systems (MIS) and in smaller shops in which programming productivity is important.

A Mainframe Monitor

An example of an expert system designed to aid computer operations is IBM's experimental YES/MVS system. This is a real-time expert system designed to interactively control an operating system. Specifically, this expert system monitors the operation of the multiple virtual storage (MVS) operating system that runs on large IBM mainframe computers. YES/MVS performs two-thirds of the operations normally handled by the computer's operator. The system was originally designed to be strictly an advisory tool for computer operators, but a later version automates many of the functions. These include managing job-entry and queue-space, monitoring network communications, preventing system crashes, monitoring software subsystems, generating reports for system programmers, scheduling large batch jobs, and monitoring the performance of the system in general.

High-speed mainframes that handle massive workloads require skilled operators to keep the system at a peak performance level. Such systems put an unusual demand on the operators because of the great volume of control messages generated by the computer and the rapid, accurate response required of the operator. An expert system monitoring the operation can detect conditions that require attention and automatically attend to them.

Program Conversion

Expert systems and other AI programs are expected to be developed to help improve programming productivity. Generating new computer programs and maintaining older ones has become more difficult and time-consuming as computing power has increased. Programming tools based on expert systems can facilitate the writing and maintaining of computer code.

Expert systems can help convert programs from one form to another, thereby lowering maintenance and programming costs.

For example, it is estimated that better than half the budget of most DP installations is devoted to maintaining existing programs. Many of these are written in reliable old COBOL. The older programs are unstructured, however, and over the years have been modified and patched to solve problems and increase capability. The result of this is known as "spaghetti code," which is difficult to maintain. Several expert systems are available to help convert these unstructured COBOL programs into structured COBOL, which is far easier to understand and modify. Initial experience with such conversions indicates that maintenance costs have been cut by 30 percent or more.

Another type of conversion program is designed to convert a program written in one language into the code of another language. These use natural language processing techniques as well as expert systems. As these programs prevent converting by hand or writing over from scratch, the resulting savings in time and programming costs are great.

Automatic Programming

One of the major hopes for AI is automatic programming. Although not a separate field of AI, automatic programming makes it possible to create expert systems and other AI programs that will replace the need for programmers to write code in specific languages. Such programs accept the programmer's definition of the input data, a description of the required processing, and the desired outputs and then produce the code necessary to run on a particular computer. This would greatly speed up and simplify the development of both small- and large-scale programs.

Expert systems can help create new software thus reducing programming time and cost.

While automatic programming is not being done today, there are many programming tools based on expert systems that automate certain programming functions. Such programming tools not only speed up software development and lower its cost, but they also enable larger, more complex programs to be developed. For example, the computer software needed to run the Strategic Defense Initiative ("Star Wars") system is so large and complex that it may take hundreds of years to create. Indeed, the complexity is such that many scientists question whether it is possible to write at all. With automated programming tools, such programs may become practical.

Data Communications

Many benefits are gained by having expert systems manage computer communications over networks.

Expert systems are expected to make a major impact in computer communications. It is common to link computers in networks so that they can share data and communicate with one another. These include small local area networks (LANs) as well as large wide area networks (WANs), which are based on the telephone system. Expert systems are being created to help network users plan, manage, and control these complex networks. For example, expert systems can help in determining the best configuration of the network to ensure the most efficient communication and to lower communications costs. As communications requirements change, reconfiguration may be necessary, and, again, expert systems can quickly determine the reconfiguration.

Expert systems are also being developed to help troubleshoot the networks. Large systems are difficult to maintain and repair because pinpointing the source of the problem takes considerable time and effort. By using expert systems, even the most complex networks can be diagnosed quickly, reducing downtime and repair costs.

Expert systems that help design new networks are also on the drawing board. The complexities of deregulation and divestiture, along with advances in technology have made designing and managing computer communications systems extremely difficult without expert help. Expert systems that integrate a wide range of knowledge and data should help in the design of efficient and trouble-free networks.

MILITARY AND GOVERNMENT APPLICATIONS

The military and numerous government organizations are now using or developing expert systems for a variety of tasks. The military leads in expert system development as it sees intelligent software as a way to improve its performance and gain competitive advantages.

The Air Force

The Air Force plans to spend millions of dollars over the next few years on various AI applications, including expert systems for air crew-aiding, target recognition, manufacturing and design.

Air crew-aiding expert systems will help pilots do their jobs more efficiently. One program, called the "Pilot's Associate," will help pilots plan their missions and alert them to threats in combat. It also monitors the aircraft subsystems for problems and informs the pilot.

A target recognition system is designed to detect and identify shapes automatically. The aircraft will contain a computer running an expert system that uses radar, infrared, and other inputs to develop a profile of distant objects. The system analyzes the profiles and attempts to identify them. While radar provides advanced warning of other aircraft, the pilot frequently cannot identify the object until it is close enough for visual contact. The target recognizer will give considerable advanced warning, providing more reaction time for the pilot.

All the services use expert systems in equipment diagnosis and repair.

The Air Force is already using expert systems to perform maintenance on combat aircraft. Most of these expert systems run on personal computers and are designed to diagnose problems in the aircraft engine and avionics. Such systems help ground maintenance personnel quickly locate and repair problems. Typically, these systems get their inputs directly from electronic sensors installed on the engine or from information extracted from the avionic equipment. These inputs pass through a cable to the computer running the expert system. The system automatically diagnoses the problem. In the avionics system, the computer may indicate the exact printed circuit board where the failure occurred. In this way, the faulty card can be changed, restoring the aircraft to operational condition.

Maintenance personnel frequently misdiagnose problems, thereby grounding aircraft for the wrong reasons. The Air Force estimates, for example, that a great percentage of electronic equipment replaced in helicopters was removed for the wrong reason. By using an expert system to make the diagnosis, such problems can be avoided.

The Air Force is also looking to expert systems to help computerize and automate the production of specialized aircraft parts. Many metal parts are produced by machine tools that run under the operation of a computer. These computers perform numerical control techniques. Instructions in the computer guide the machine tool in grinding, cutting, and otherwise shaping the metal into the desired part. By building expert systems for decision making into the software, the Air Force expects that parts' quality will improve. Such expert systems eliminate the need for human operators who often slow or stop the production process. By having the computers assess problems and decide on corrective action, higher production and lower costs are projected.

Some advanced applications of expert systems in the Air Force are directed at the Strategic Defense Initiative (SDI), which is being designed as a defensive shield against nuclear war. Because of the size and complexity of the system, computers, and expert systems, will play a major role in automating system operation. Their primary application will be in the battle management segment, which uses computers for assembling information about a situation from satellite-based radars, infrared detectors, and other sensors, evaluating that information, considering various alternative courses of action, and making a final determination on how to proceed.

The Army

The Army is just beginning to use expert systems. The average soldier on the battlefield is responsible for a huge territory and, therefore, must have the best information, advice, and communications available. Expert systems promise to give the soldier a strategic advantage.

Like the other services, the Army is building expert systems to diagnose equipment problems. Expert systems are being built for weapons, transportation vehicles, and communications systems. By using expert systems to improve the ability to maintain and repair

With today's high-tech warfare, the Army has to do more with fewer soldiers in less time and make fewer mistakes.

equipment, maintenance costs should be reduced and equipment preparedness increased. An example of such an expert system is one designed to help diagnose technical problems in the M-1 tank. This high-tech fighting machine has dozens of subsystems and thousands of electrical connections. Weapons this complex are difficult to repair, especially during wartime. Anything that can expedite the process is a real advantage.

Expert systems will help reduce the human information overload condition that occurs in battle.

A major effort is underway by a number of organizations to build battlefield management expert systems that will help field commanders make critical decisions. During battle, inputs from reconnaissance teams and intelligence gathering groups are fed to a central location where they are analyzed to determine the status of the battle. Most intelligence analysts are overburdened with data and, at the same time, they are required to process it and produce reports under tight deadlines. As we have seen, expert systems are ideal in those situations where humans are in overload. Providing the intelligence data to expert systems allows an assessment of the situation to be made quickly and reliably.

The most important part of such a system is threat analysis, where multiple information sources provide the data that the expert system uses to determine whether a threat exists and, if so, its magnitude. Other expert systems provide situation assessments and can help formulate battle plans. While such expert systems are not currently operational, their development is being expedited.

The Army is investigating other applications of AI, such as the potential of smart robots to pick up and deliver materials in the field. Another research project is the autonomous land vehicle designed to use AI techniques to seek out enemy locations and carry out a variety of tasks. The idea is to create special weapons and vehicles that can operate autonomously with their own native intelligence rather than risking lives. These projects involve computer vision as well as expert systems.

Expert systems will also be a part of the Army's command, control, communications, and intelligence (C3I) systems. These integrated communications and computer systems are designed to provide optimum communications and intelligence for battlefield commanders.

The Army is also beginning to use expert systems in non-warfare–related applications. As an example, the Army logistics center has created an expert system that helps determine how many support personnel are required in newly established units. An expert system derived from available Army regulation manuals helps determine personnel requirements for quartermaster and supply services. These regulations have been boiled down into a concise knowledge base that is designed to apply the regulations consistently. It is expected that significant personnel and monetary savings can be achieved.

The Navy

The Navy's applications of expert systems parallel those of the other services. Expert systems for battle management at sea are under development and testing. Like the other services, the Navy is using expert systems for the diagnosis and repair of weapons and communications systems. The Navy is also beginning to use expert systems in budget analysis. Navy budgets are large and complex and require numerous analysts to determine their content and make good decisions based on priorities. The result should be improved budget decisions with fewer analysts involved.

The Government

As you might expect, expert systems offer the potential to improve productivity and decision-making processes in almost every area of government. While expert systems are not in wide use throughout government, many agencies are examining their potential and developing pilot programs. We'll look at some examples to get a feel for the kinds of uses to which expert systems may be put.

The Department of Energy is studying AI and expert systems as general problem-solving tools. One system is designed to aid inspectors as they study power plant installations in order to decide on their suitability.

The Environmental Protection Agency is looking at expert systems as a way to assist in writing projects. For example, the EPA issues permits to organizations involved in discharging water into lakes and rivers. The water discharged must be free of toxic pollutants. The EPA has a tremendous backlog of such permits simply because it does not have enough personnel with the expertise to evaluate and approve them. An expert system embodying the knowledge of those qualified to analyze applications and issue permits will be packaged into an expert system. This should reduce the backlog and allow permits to be issued in a timely manner.

The Federal Aviation Agency is also investigating expert systems as a way to improve air traffic control and flight safety in general. An example is an expert system that helps air traffic controllers ensure that aircraft in high-traffic areas are safely separated from one another. The number of incidents of near misses is increasing and there is great concern over the possibility of more mid-air collisions. Again, the expert system will help the air traffic controllers, who work in an overloaded condition.

The Federal Emergency Management Agency is considering the use of expert systems for advice in dealing with major national catastrophes. These include natural phenomena such as earthquakes and storms as well as emergencies such as war and physical disasters. The FEMA currently uses decision support systems on computers to help in emergency management situations. Expert systems promise to greatly improve the agency's ability to deal with emergency situations, perhaps even helping mitigate the impact of the hazard. They might also help in preparedness by resolving issues with regard to the positioning of various resources for emergency use. Expert systems would also help in situation assessment and critical resource allocation. Overall, expert systems would greatly improve the management and decision-making ability of the FEMA during a time of crisis.

The FBI and NASA are also using or planning to use expert systems. The FBI uses expert systems in conjunction with the large computer data bases to help investigators and field agents research clues and draw inferences about crimes. NASA uses expert systems on the space shuttle and expects to use them on the space station coming in the 1990s. The intelligence agencies are undoubtedly taking maximum advantage of expert systems.

OTHER USES

We have only scratched the surface in this chapter. There are just too many potential uses for expert systems to cover them all here. There are expert systems for use in agriculture, chemistry, oil exploration, law, meteorology, physics, process control, education; any field in which expert knowledge can be captured and applied is a candidate for application.

There are few real expert systems in use because they are difficult to develop.

The great number and variety of expert systems discussed in this chapter may give you the impression that there are hundreds or even thousands of practical systems in daily use. That is not yet the case. In reality, there are precious few in use. The technology is still relatively new, and many have yet to discover it, much less adopt it. Expert systems are also difficult and time-consuming to create. While a simple system may take six months to a year to create, more comprehensive systems may take years to develop and perfect. Many expert systems are under development now so there will be many new ones in the future, but for a while yet they will be scarce.

What Have We Learned?

1. Expert systems usually employ heuristic knowledge to solve problems. Knowledge-based systems use knowledge from books and other sources.

2. Expert and knowledge-based systems are often referred to as consultation systems because they provide advice much as human consultants do.

3. The main uses of expert systems in business and government are for troubleshooting and intelligent alternative selection.

4. Financial expert systems add a new dimension to managing all aspects of money. Banks, tax and accounting firms, stock and bond brokers, insurance companies, and financial planners all use expert systems.

5. Diagnostic expert systems are widely used to help expedite repair of complex equipment. This minimizes downtime, speeds maintenance, lowers troubleshooting costs, and enables less-experienced personnel to repair sophisticated systems.

6. Medical expert systems diagnose diseases, helping physicians apply treatment sooner, and the expert systems diagnose unusual illnesses outside of physicians' normal expertise.

7. Expert systems are added to traditional algorithmic and simulation computer-aided design systems to help engineers create more sophisticated designs and to speed up designs of printed circuit boards and VLSI chips.

8. Manufacturing expert systems help companies produce more and higher-quality goods in less time at lower costs. They assist managers in planning better work flow, identify areas for improvement, and expedite configuration and troubleshooting.

9. Expert systems are gaining favor with DP and MIS managers because they help improve the operating efficiency of mainframes, lower software development and maintenance costs, and help manage data communications.

10. Military expert systems help provide a strategic advantage over the enemy by assisting in battle assessment and management, automating weapons, troubleshooting and repair of weapons, and increasing the capabilities of the combatants.

11. Government agencies, traditionally heavy users of computers, are discovering many creative uses for expert systems.

12. Expert systems' usage is as broad as that of computers in general. Virtually any field in which expert knowledge can be packaged and applied to some benefit is a candidate.

13. There are few real-world expert systems in use today because the technology is still relatively new and expert systems are difficult and time-consuming to develop.

Quiz for Chapter 3

1. AI software that contains the knowledge of books, journals, and other written sources is referred to as a(n):
   a. expert system.
   b. knowledge system.
   c. advisory system.
   d. consultant system.

2. Expert systems are characterized by their use of:
   a. textbook knowledge.
   b. common sense.
   c. heuristic knowledge from experience.
   d. a data base.

3. Which of the following is *not* one of the main uses of expert systems?
   a. Control of systems.
   b. Selection of best alternative.
   c. Diagnostic/troubleshooting.

4. Which of the following is *not* a major use of financial expert systems?
   a. Loan decisions.
   b. Tax advice.
   c. Financial planning.
   d. General ledger accounting.

5. Which of the following organizations use expert systems?
   a. Insurance companies.
   b. Banks.
   c. Stock brokers.
   d. All of the above.

6. Expert systems are good at diagnosing problems in:
   a. home appliances.
   b. cars.
   c. complex electronic systems.
   d. all of the above.

7. Expert systems are vital in many diagnostic applications because:
   a. downtime is expensive and intolerable.
   b. there are many repairpeople to replace.
   c. repairpeople are scarce.
   d. repair costs are too expensive.

8. A medical expert system that acts like a top-notch internist is:
   a. CADUCEUS.
   b. MYCIN.
   c. PUFF.
   d. HELP.

9. Expert systems are becoming a part of software packages that help engineers create new products. This software is called:
   a. simulation.
   b. design aids.
   c. computer-aided design.
   d. spreadsheets.

10. Expert systems help management achieve such manufacturing goals as:
    a. higher productivity.
    b. higher quality.
    c. lower costs.
    d. all of the above.

11. A goal of expert system software developers is:
 a. language-to-language translation.
 b. automatic programming.
 c. operating system monitoring.
 d. data communications management.

12. All military services use expert systems for:
 a. diagnosis and repair.
 b. logistics support.
 c. manufacturing.
 d. target recognition.

13. Virtually all fields can use expert systems as long as they:
 a. have lots of data to process.
 b. have knowledge to apply.
 c. use large computers.
 d. have enough money.

Knowledge Representation and Search

ABOUT THIS CHAPTER

The heart of any expert system is its knowledge base. The knowledge of one or more experts is boiled down to form a data base that is accessed by the inference program when solving problems. The primary concern of those building expert systems is how to represent knowledge inside a computer. We have already seen that knowledge representation is symbolic. However, we'll take that one step farther in this chapter and examine in some detail just how the heuristic knowledge of an expert is translated into a form that the computer can use.

Knowledge representation is a major subfield of AI research. While many useful techniques have been discovered and perfected, the search goes on for better ways to represent knowledge. Essentially, knowledge representation establishes convenient organizing formats. In this chapter, we will introduce you to the more popular ways of representing knowledge in expert systems. These include production rules, frames, semantic networks, and examples.

We will also introduce you to *search*, the basic problem-solving method in AI. As the inference program looks through the knowledge base seeking answers, it examines the "chunks" of knowledge, trying to find a match to a fact. The methods of search are called "control strategies." We'll examine these as we go along.

TYPES OF KNOWLEDGE

A knowledge base can use two kinds of knowledge—declarative and procedural.

Two basic kinds of knowledge can be put into a knowledge base: declarative knowledge and procedural knowledge. Most expert systems will contain both.

Declarative Knowledge

Declarative knowledge, also called "descriptive" knowledge, is primarily a statement of fact about people, places, or things. Declarative knowledge permits you to state information, deduce relationships, and classify objects. Using declarative knowledge you cannot explain anything, but you can present truths and their association with each other. In expert systems, declarative knowledge representation schemes include semantic networks, frames, and production rules.

Procedural Knowledge

Procedural or *prescriptive* knowledge, is explanatory; it provides a way of applying the declarative knowledge. With this kind of knowledge, you can show procedures for performing a course of action. Procedural knowledge recommends what to do and how. A list of instructions for installing a program on a hard disk storage unit and a step-by-step sequence for disassembling a large electric motor are both examples of procedural knowledge. Procedural knowledge is represented in expert systems as production rules and scripts.

PRODUCTION RULES

The common method of representing knowledge in expert systems is with production rules. Production rules, sometimes referred to as "rules" or "productions," are two-part statements that contain a small increment of knowledge. The domain, or subject, to be represented in an expert system is divided up into many small chunks of knowledge. The knowledge is usually heuristic, which is easily represented in rule format. Expert systems using production rules are sometimes called "production systems," and the knowledge base is sometimes called the "rule base." All production systems are expert systems, but not all expert systems are production systems because there are forms of knowledge representation other than production rules.

Rule Format

A rule is a two-part statement containing a premise and a conclusion.

The two parts of a rule are a premise and a conclusion, a situation and an action, or an antecedent and a consequent. These statements are written in an *IF-THEN* format. The first part of the rule, generally called the "left-hand" part, is prefaced by the word *IF*, to state a situation or premise. The second or "right-hand" part of the rule is prefaced with *THEN* to state an action or a conclusion. Production rules are simple to understand and use and are ideally suited to a wide range of heuristic knowledge. Most knowledge domains are easily represented in this format. Some examples of rules are shown here.

1. IF   the water level exceeds 4 feet
   THEN start the pump.

2. IF   the fish has a triangular top fin
   THEN it is a shark.

Some types of knowledge require a more complex rule, such as this:

3. IF   the fruit is red
   AND has seeds
   AND grows on a vine
   THEN it is a tomato.

In this rule, the premise or situation begins with an IF but also contains two AND statements that are part of the situation or premise. If the conclusion is to be true, then all three statements in the premise must be true. As many additional AND statements may be used as are required to represent a desired piece of knowledge.

Another way to make a knowledge statement is to use OR statements in the premise. Along with the initial statement, one or more OR statements may also be included.

4. IF   the switch is off
   OR   the fuse is blown
   THEN the circuit will be off.

In rules of this type, the conclusion stated in the THEN part of the rule will be true IF any one or more of the statements in the premise is true. This format provides a flexible way of representing some types of knowledge. More complex rules may include AND and OR statements.

Since rules represent only tiny increments of knowledge, it takes a considerable number of them to represent the knowledge of a particular domain. Small expert systems may have only ten or twenty rules but the more useful systems usually have well over a hundred. Large systems have many thousands of rules.

The main benefit of rules is that they facilitate creation, modification, and maintenance of a knowledge base because the knowledge is modularized. Since much domain knowledge changes over time, new rules must be added and old rules removed or modified to keep the knowledge base current. With rules, these changes can be made quickly and easily.

Measures of Confidence

We mentioned earlier that AI software is capable of dealing with ambiguity and uncertainty. Algorithmic software is not. An algorithm, such as a formula, needs specific input values supplied before it can compute an output. If you give it proper inputs, it will generate a correct output. Of course, if the inputs are wrong, you can expect to get an incorrect output and thus the old expression "Garbage in, garbage out."

AI software, however, doesn't always need perfect inputs and outputs in order to be useful. When the expert system you are using asks you questions, you may not be able to supply the desired answers. In some cases, you will not know the answers at all. There will be other times when you have answers but you're unsure of their validity. Most expert systems are designed to be able to deal with these situations.

Certainty Factors

One method that has been devised to deal with uncertainty is *certainty factors*. A certainty factor (CF) is a numerical measure of the confidence you have in the validity of a fact or rule. It allows the inferencing program to work with inexact information.

A variety of certainty factor scales can be used. Some of these are illustrated in *Figure 4-1*. The most often used is a scale from 0 to 1 where 0 indicates a total lack of confidence and 1 represents complete confidence. Other expert systems may use such scales as 0 to 10 or 0 to 100. You can also use a −1 to +1 scale as *Figure 4-1* shows. Other arbitrary arrangements may be set up by a programmer. Here is a rule for using certainty factors:

IF   the regulator output is zero

AND   the regulator input is correct

THEN the regulator circuit is defective (.9).

This rule states that we are pretty sure that if the input is good but the output is zero, then the problem is in the regulator. But we don't give the conclusion a 1.0 confidence rating because there could conceivably be a less common problem, say a broken wire or defective connector.

While the programmer sets up the CF scale, the expert actually puts the correct value on the rule. Only the expert knows just how confident he or she is in the rule's outcome because certainty factors are nothing more than intelligent guesses based

Figure 4-1.
Examples of Certainty
Scales

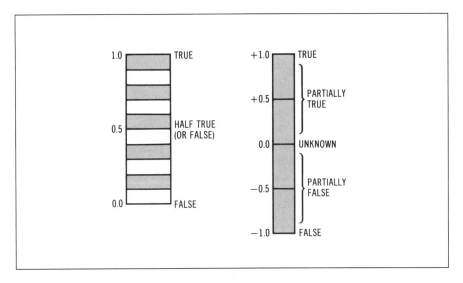

upon experience and available statistical data. The expert sets the certainty factors when constructing the knowledge base, but they may have to be changed when the system's validity is tested.

The expert system usually reaches a conclusion based on several rules in a chain. If each rule or conclusion has a CF, the outcome will have a composite CF. Several methods have been devised for combining certainty factors. One of these is indicated here.

$$CF(C) = CF(A) + CF(B) - CF(A) \times CF(B)$$

The certainty factor of the conclusion or outcome (C) depends upon the certainty factors of rules A and B, as we see here:

Rule A: IF   X
           AND   Y
           THEN   Z(CF = .75).

Rule B: IF   D
           AND   E
           THEN   F(CF = .3).

$$
\begin{aligned}
CF(C) &= CF(A) + CF(B) - CF(A) \times CF(B) \\
&= .75 + .3 - (.75)(.3) \\
&= 1.05 - .225 \\
&= .825
\end{aligned}
$$

Probability

It is important to understand that a certainty factor is not the same thing as *probability*. A CF is just a number on an arbitrary scale that states to what extent we believe the knowledge is true. Probability, on the other hand, is a number that indicates the chance of an action occurring or not occurring. Probability (P) is the ratio of the number of times that an event (X) occurs to the total number of events (N) that take place. Mathematically, this is expressed as:

$$P = X/N$$

For example, when you roll a die, you know that there is one chance in six of the die landing on a particular number. If the die is perfectly balanced and it is thrown a great number of times, each of the six sides would eventually show up one-sixth of the time. The chance of rolling a two, for example, expressed mathematically is simply:

$$P(2) = \frac{1}{6} = .16666, \text{ or about } 16.7\% \text{ of the time}$$

Depending upon the type of knowledge involved, probability may be a more suitable way to deal with uncertainty than certainty factors so some expert systems use probability rather than certainty factors. In general, these are harder to implement.

One popular kind of probability calculation is Bayes' theorem or rule. This Bayesian probability is a formula that computes the probability of event X occurring if event Y has already occurred. In probability math terminology, this is P(X:Y). It is computed with the expression:

$$P(X:Y) = \frac{P(Y:X)P(X)}{P(Y:X)P(X)} + P(Y:\text{not } X)P(\text{not } X)$$

P(not X) means the probability of X not occurring and is simply equal to $1-P(X)$ or 1 minus the probability that X does occur. P(Y:X) means the probability of Y occurring, given that X has already occurred.

Stringing such calculations along in a big system where a lot of rules are evaluated to reach a conclusion causes a lot of computing to take place, slowing down the process. Despite its complexity, such an approach works if warranted. The PROSPECTOR expert system for locating mineral deposits uses this approach.

Fuzzy Logic

One method of handling imprecise knowledge is a mathematical system called "fuzzy logic." An expert, when creating the knowledge base, may wish to use imprecise terms such as short and long or large and small. The expert assigns a value between 0 and 1 to such a quantity, indicating the degree of possibility that it is within a given range.

Assume you wish to define what a fast car is. Although you might use top speed as a measure, few cars ever hit top speed, so a better measure might be 0 to 60 miles per hour (mph) acceleration time. Say that any car with a time for 0 to 60 mph less than eight seconds is fast and all others are slow. We could show this graphically as in *Figure 4-2a*. The vertical scale represents the opinions of experts on what is fast. The rating 1.0 means that 100 percent think below 8 seconds is fast. The 0 means no one believes any above 8 seconds is fast.

Of course, there is rarely such concensus. In real life, the experts' opinions would probably differ, so a more realistic curve might be like that in *Figure 4-2b*. This shows that only 50 percent of the experts think a time below 8 seconds is fast. In any case, the number between 0 and 1 gives you a value that expresses the fastness of a car rated by experts over the given ranges. Those figures might also represent such conditions as large, true, rich, ugly, or sinful; they can be helpful in reasoning with "fuzzy" data.

This method of representing imprecise information is useful for some types of problems. It enables us to assign a numerical value to knowledge whose validity is not known. Numerical values are required, of course, if a computer program is going to process and evaluate the knowledge.

Certainty factors are by far the most widely used method to represent confidence levels in rule-based expert systems. Most expert system development tools that allow you to build expert systems without programming use certainty factors. Probability and fuzzy logic are not as widely used (although fuzzy logic is growing in popularity), but these methods fit some problems better than certainty factors.

SEMANTIC NETWORKS

A semantic network is a graphical depiction of knowledge about objects and relationships.

One of the simplest and most effective ways to represent certain types of knowledge is to use a *semantic network* or semantic net. A semantic net is a graphical representation of knowledge that shows the relationship between objects. Semantic networks are excellent for representing declarative knowledge, particularly that which has a hierarchical structure. When the knowledge can be classified or categorized, it is a good candidate for a semantic net.

**Figure 4-2.
Fuzzy Logic Curves for
"Fast" Car**

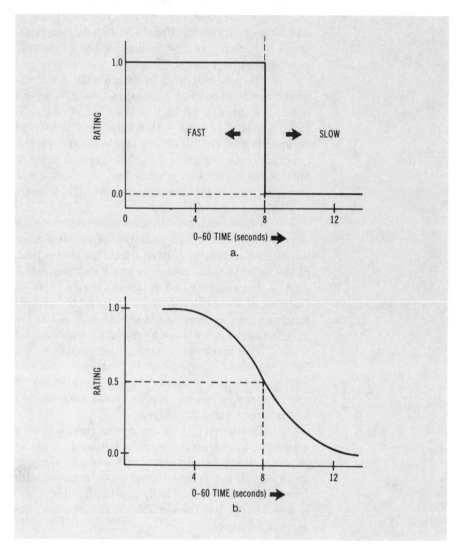

An example of a semantic network is shown in *Figure 4-3*. The circles are called "nodes" and are used to represent people, places, things, or ideas. The nodes are connected to one another to show relationships. These links between nodes are called "arcs." On each arc is a label that states the relationship between the nodes that it connects. While semantic networks are an excellent visual tool, they can also be programmed into a computer to form a complete knowledge base.

**Figure 4-3.
A Semantic Network**

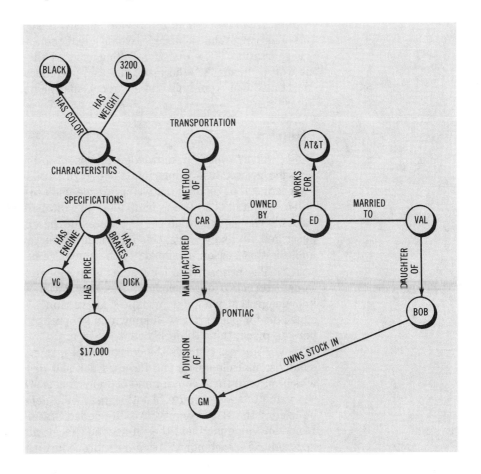

By referring to the semantic network in *Figure 4-3*, you can see that most nodes represent an object, but that other nodes represent attributes of the related object, such as size, color, or specification.

An important characteristic of a semantic network is that some nodes may inherit properties or characteristics from other nodes. Since semantic nets are used to represent hierarchical information, some nodes will be higher in the hierarchy than others. Nodes that are lower in the hierarchy can inherit properties from the nodes higher in the network. This characteristic of a semantic network eliminates the need to repeat information at each node.

To solve problems with a semantic network, you ask questions about the domain being represented. The inferencing program searches through the various arcs and nodes looking for the key words in the question. If the knowledge is built into the system, it would be able to provide specific answers. For example, the question "What is a car?" would yield the answer "method of transportation." The question "What color is the car?" would be answered "black." "Who made the car?" would be answered "Pontiac." GM would also be a correct answer because of inheritance.

FRAMES

The *frame* is a knowledge representation scheme that is growing in use. It is primarily designed to handle declarative knowledge. For example, a frame can be used to describe any object in detail. The frame is divided into discrete elements called "slots." The slots contain the attributes of the object being described. In many ways, this knowledge structure is hierarchical and, for that reason, is similar to the semantic network.

A frame formats stereotyped knowledge about objects.

The primary use for frames is to represent what is referred to as "stereotyped knowledge." Stereotyped knowledge is knowledge that we know or expect about things. Frames are excellent for packaging well-known or generalized attributes of any person, place, thing, object, event, or idea.

Figure 4-4 shows the concept of a frame. It is made up of subdivisions called slots and facets. Each slot describes an attribute, which may, in turn, contain one or more facets. One facet may be the value of the attribute. Another may be a *default* value that can be used if the slot is empty. An "if-needed" facet may also be used. If no slot value is given, the "if-needed" facet, also called a "procedural attachment," triggers a procedure that goes out and gets or computes a value.

Figure 4-5 shows a frame for IBM's PC/2 computer. All of the slots are filled with specific values for each attribute, except for the operating system and performance slots. A default value for the operating system is PC DOS 3.3, but the larger, multitasking OS/2 can also be used. The performance slot is filled by a procedural attachment that will go out and run a benchmark to obtain a numerical value that expresses performance in a way that it can be compared to similar computers.

Since frames are similar to semantic networks because they are excellent for dealing with hierarchical knowledge, you might expect that multiple frames could be linked. And you'd be right.

Figure 4-4.
Basic Format of Frame
Representation

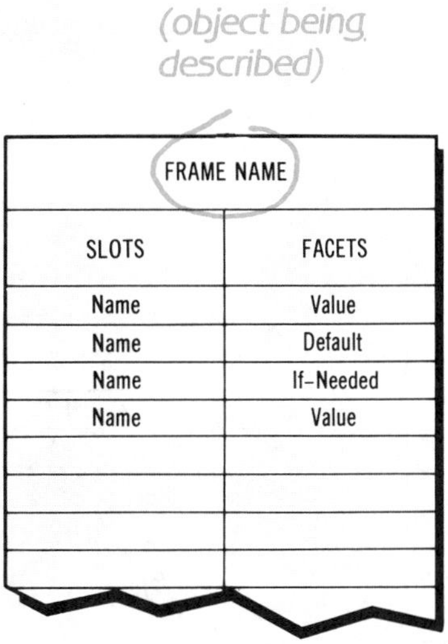

(object being described)

FRAME NAME	
SLOTS	**FACETS**
Name	Value
Name	Default
Name	If–Needed
Name	Value

Figure 4-5.
Frame Describing a
Personal Computer

PC/2 MODEL 50	
SLOTS	**FACETS**
Type	Personal Computer
Manufacturer	IBM
Model	PC/2 Model 50
Processor	80286
RAM	1 MB
Floppy disk size	3.5″
Hard disk	20 MB
Expansion slots	3
Video monitor	14″ color RGB
Operating system	PC DOS 3.3 (default)
Performance	Procedural Attachment

Frames may be interconnected just like semantic networks to form an incredibly detailed knowledge base. A particular slot in a frame may reference another frame that contains detailed information about that particular attribute. A slot in that second frame then could reference another and so on. This concept is illustrated in *Figure 4-6.*

Figure 4-6.
Linking Frames to
Create More Detailed
Knowledge Bases

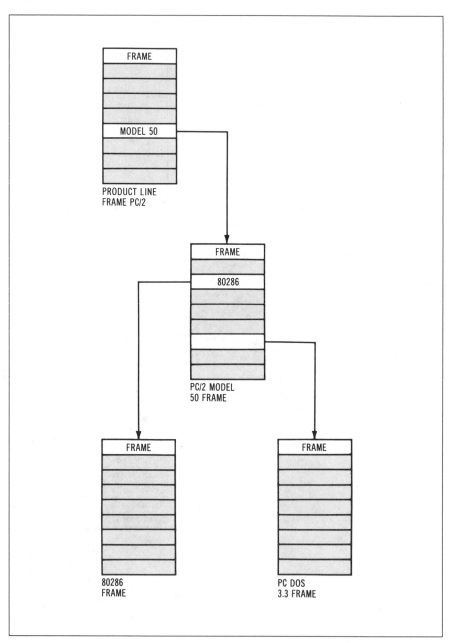

A slot in this product line frame refers to the Model 50 frame given in *Figure 4-5*. In turn, it refers to detailed frames for the 80286 microprocessor and PC DOS 3.3.

When frames are linked together in a hierarchy, as in *Figure 4-6*, one frame may inherit the properties of a higher-level frame. As with semantic networks, this ability of frames to inherit properties makes knowledge storage more compact and permits in-depth reasoning. As with other forms of knowledge representation, inferencing is done by detailed search of the slots and frames.

EXAMPLES

One of the simplest ways to format knowledge is to state examples about problem-solving in the domain.

One way to impart knowledge to an expert system is to state a number of examples or case histories about the domain. You can do this by listing the conclusions, outcomes, or answers that the expert system is expected to give. Then for each of these, designate the attributes required to cause that outcome to be selected. The easiest way to do this is to set up a matrix like that for troubleshooting an electronic power supply shown in *Figure 4-7*.

Figure 4-7.
Matrix of Examples

	AC VOLTAGE IN	TRANSFORMER SECONDARY VOLTAGE	FILTER OUTPUT/ REGULATOR INPUT	REGULATOR OUTPUT	SUSPECTED CAUSE
1.	Ok	Ok	Normal	Zero	Defective Regulator
2.	Ok	Ok	Low	Low	Defective Filter Capacitor
3.	Ok	Ok	Zero	Zero	Defective Rectifier
4.	Ok	Zero	Zero	Zero	Fuse Blown

The matrix provides a convenient format of rows and columns that can be filled in. All of the possible outcomes or conclusions are given in the right-most column. Each row of the matrix contains the attributes that lead to that conclusion.

Many expert system development tools use this form of knowledge representation by example. The matrix format provides a simple framework for setting up the knowledge. But while the format may be examples in a matrix, the knowledge base itself usually takes on a different form. What happens is that a program in the expert system converts the examples into rules. In other words, given the matrix of examples, the expert system deduces its own rules to form the knowledge base. The rules are used by the inference program to draw conclusions. Later in this book we examine an expert system that uses this technique.

SEARCH TECHNIQUES

The basic problem-solving method used in artificial intelligence is *search*. Search, as its name implies, is the process of examining a large set of possible solutions to a problem in an attempt to find the best solution. This is a trial-and-error method of looking through a knowledge base attempting to match knowledge items to known facts. The knowledge base, referred to as the "search space," comprises all final solutions to the problem and any intermediate solutions. In a real-world expert system, the search space is usually a set of IF THEN rules, and it might also be the nodes and arcs of a semantic network or a collection of frames.

Search techniques, or *inferencing control strategies*, are one of the major research fields in AI. New methods to speed up and otherwise improve the search process are constantly sought. Despite the apparently simple nature of the search process, many sophisticated techniques have been devised to make this method of problem-solving practical on a computer. In this section we want to introduce the basic concepts of search and examine those methods most widely used in expert systems.

Search Trees

A *search tree* is a graphical method of representing the search space. In order to visualize the elements of knowledge in a knowledge base, a picture can be drawn using nodes and arcs like those in semantic networks. Each node represents one fact, rule, or another knowledge element. The nodes are interconnected with arcs showing the relationships. The resulting diagram often looks like an inverted tree, with roots and trunk at the top and the branches and leaves spread out toward the bottom. A typical search tree is shown in *Figure 4-8*.

**Figure 4-8.
A Search Tree**

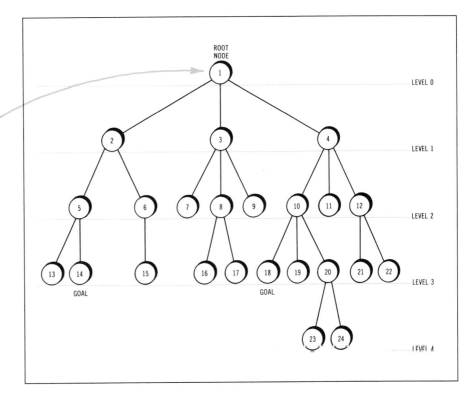

The initial state of the search process is referred to as the "root node." Growing downward from the root node, the branches extend to *successor* nodes, which are also called "children." Each additional node has one or more successors. Eventually the bottom nodes in the tree have no children.

The basic structure of a search tree is hierarchical, and it is similar to an organizational chart. As we see in the figure, the levels of nodes are numbered to make them easier to identify.

In most practical AI software, including expert systems, the search space is far too large to draw the search tree for a knowledge base. For that reason, search trees are rarely drawn to depict a problem, but the concept helps explain how an inference engine searches through a knowledge base. You can assume that the search tree exists or you might imagine the search space growing, an increment at a time, as the inference engine moves from one node to the next, looking for a solution.

Decision Trees

A decision tree lists alternative decisions or paths to a goal or solution.

Like a search tree, a *decision tree* has a root node, intermediate nodes, connecting arcs, and goals. The two terms—search and decision tree—are often used interchangeably. In a decision tree, though, each node represents a decision point. For example, at node 3 in *Figure 4-8*, there are three possible decisions, nodes 7, 8, and 9. Node 8 has two decisions, nodes 16 and 17. You can consider each node to be a question with one or more answers.

Figure 4-9 shows a simple decision tree that leads to a choice of some type of transportation. At each node, a decision is made. A simple form of decision tree has two paths for each node, yes and no or true and false. Despite the simplicity of such a tree, there are many applications that naturally fit this arrangement or can be set up to use this format.

Figure 4-9.
A Decision Tree

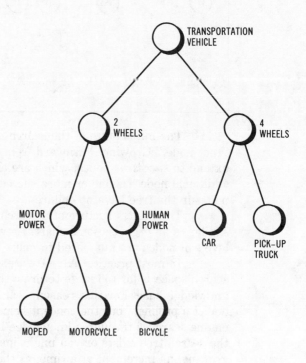

Blind Search and Combinatorial Explosion

Blind search is a brute-force method that examines all nodes until the solution is found.

Blind search is a brute-force method of looking through every node in the search tree seeking a solution. Blind search examines the entire search tree in an orderly manner in an effort to draw a conclusion. The blind search starts with the root node and then systematically works its way downward in the search tree from left to right.

Blind search is reliable but slow.

While blind search is practically guaranteed to produce a solution, its disadvantage is that it is a slow, tedious process. Keep in mind that the basic search process is one of looking through the knowledge base stored in a computer's memory and comparing elements of it to known facts in a data base. At each node, the computer must do some pattern-matching, where rules, frames, or portions of them are compared to a data string representing a fact to be verified. When a large search tree is involved, the search for a solution can sometimes occupy a considerable amount of time. While modern computers operate at very high speeds, a blind search of a large search tree may produce unacceptably long computing times. While we are used to computer response times in fractions of a second and certainly no more than several seconds, a complex search could take minutes or even hours. The solution is to find a still faster computer or to limit the search. A great deal of research in AI is focused on this process of narrowing research and thus cutting the time required.

As the number of nodes and levels in a tree increases, the number of search alternatives grows exponentially.

You can understand why it is important to develop techniques for limiting the search when you consider the awesome number of alternatives that must be examined in a very large search tree. You can compute the total number of possible solutions in a search tree mathematically. If each node in a search tree has n branches to other nodes and the tree has d levels (the root node is not considered a level), the total number of nodes in the search space is computed by raising n to the d power.

$$\text{TOTAL NODES} = n^d$$

The greater the number of nodes and the more branches per node, the more quickly the tree expands. This mathematical expansion is referred to as combinatorial explosion. A tree can become so large as to make blind search an unacceptable approach to problem-solving.

For example, a tree with 3 levels and 3 branches per level has 3 raised to the third power or $3 \times 3 \times 3 = 27$ possible solution nodes. But consider a tree with 9 levels of 6 branches each. It has 10,077,696 outcomes!

Search Strategies

There are four basic ways to go about examining a search tree. These methods determine the order in which the nodes in the tree are examined: breadth-first search, depth-first search, forward search, and backward search.

Breadth-First Search

A breadth-first search begins at the root node and continues downward, looking at all of the nodes at a level before going to the next lower level. As illustrated in *Figure 4-10*, the breadth-first search, indicated numerically on the figure, examines all of the nodes on one level from left to right before progressing to the next lower level. This search would end at node 14, the first goal.

Figure 4-10.
Breadth-First Search

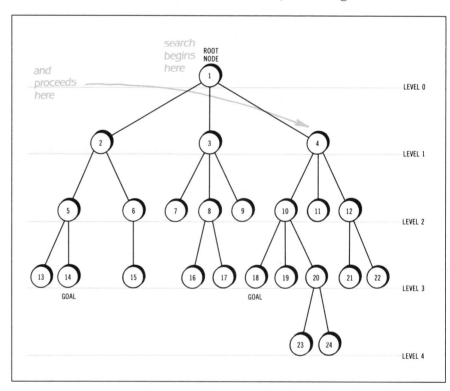

Depth-First Search

The depth-first search begins at the root node and then works its way down through the various levels to the deepest possible node in the left-most branch. If the final node in a branch isn't a goal, the search backtracks through the previous node or nodes until it reaches a point where it can move downward again. The search process continues left to right in this manner until a solution is found. The depth-first search process is illustrated in *Figure 4-11*. The search sequence follows the numerical labels and ends at node 5, the first goal encountered.

**Figure 4-11.
Depth-First Search**

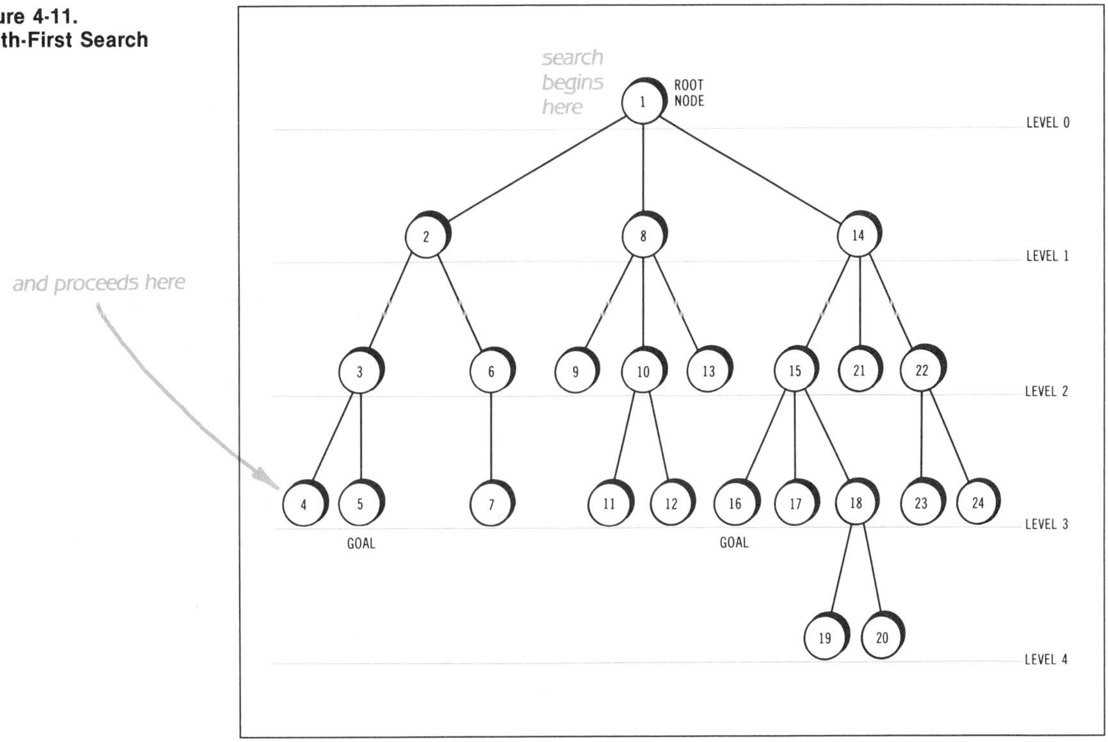

Forward Search

Forward search, also called "forward-reasoning" or "forward-chaining," begins with the root node and searches downward into the tree until a goal or solution node is found. In other words, forward search encompasses both breadth- and depth-first search. Forward search begins with a fact and moves forward, attempting to match that fact to nodes in the knowledge base. Forward search is said to be data driven.

Backward Search

The preferred control strategy in most expert systems is backward search.

In backward search, also called "backward-reasoning" or "backward-chaining," the search begins at the goal node. One way to solve a problem is to assume a particular goal or outcome and then to search for evidence that supports or proves that goal. *Figure 4-12* shows one possible backward-chaining search sequence. This is a depth-first approach, but a breadth-first approach could also be used. Note that there are multiple goals as well as several root nodes. Some problems may fit this model. Should the search based on one goal fail, then the search continues by selecting another goal and then attempting to find facts that support that outcome. This kind of search is said to be goal directed and simulates a kind of inductive reasoning. The search may backtrack as required to find the proof for the selected goal.

Figure 4-12.
A Backward-Chaining
Search Sequence

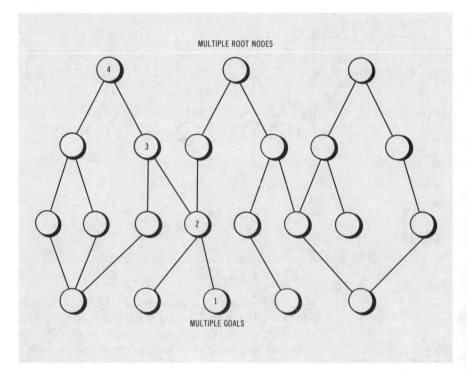

Both forward- and backward-chaining are widely used techniques in expert system search. Backward reasoning is probably more widely used than forward reasoning, although you'll find both systems used extensively. The search strategy is chosen to fit the kind of problem being solved. Further, some systems use a combination of forward- and backward-chaining that can help reduce search time, speeding the problem solving. Later, when we discuss expert system operation, we will again consider forward- and backward-chaining techniques.

Heuristic Search

Heuristic techniques make the search process more efficient and faster.

Previously we used "heuristic" to describe a rule of thumb that helps to express knowledge. But, the term can also refer to techniques that are used to limit a search. Heuristics are ways of focusing on only those portions of the search tree most likely to yield a solution. Heuristic techniques can eliminate large portions of the search tree, thus greatly accelerating problem solution.

There are general-purpose heuristics and domain-specific heuristics. An example of a general-purpose search heuristic is *depth-bound* search. This technique is used in depth-first searches to help eliminate the possibility that the search will go off into some deep network of branches where there may be no possibility for solution. A depth-bound search arbitrarily limits the depth of the search to some maximum level. It cuts off the search process at that point, forcing backtracking. The difficulty, of course, is in knowing at what level to set the boundary so that potential solutions are not eliminated.

Domain-specific heuristics are applicable only to certain types of problems. One type of domain-specific heuristic is the use of special rules, called "meta rules," that state ways that the knowledge rules can be used. If a meta rule is true given certain input facts, it will limit the search to a subset of the knowledge base containing rules that will most likely lead to the solution. With this approach, you create a small knowledge base about how to guide search processes in the most efficient way.

Another way to minimize the search process is to subdivide the problem and the knowledge base into a hierarchy. In this way, the search can be constricted to those portions of the hierarchy most likely to lead to a rapid solution.

What Have We Learned?

1. The basic problem-solving strategy in AI is search and pattern-matching in a knowledge base by an inferencing program.

2. A major concern in AI is knowledge representation. There are numerous ways to organize and format knowledge to create a rule base in the desired domain.

3. There are two basic types of knowledge, declarative and procedural. Declarative knowledge includes statements or descriptions of facts about objects and their relationships. Procedural knowledge explains methods of doing things.

4. The most widely used form of knowledge representation in expert systems is the production rule. A production rule has two parts, the IF that states a premise or condition and the THEN that expresses a corresponding conclusion or action.

5. Inexact, ambiguous, or uncertain knowledge may be handled in expert systems by using certainty factors, probability, or fuzzy logic.

6. A semantic network is a graphical method of showing knowledge that is made up of nodes representing people, places, things, or events connected by arcs, which show associations.

7. A frame is a scheme for showing stereotyped knowledge as a list of slots filled with the values of attributes about the object. Frames may be linked to provide more detailed knowledge.

8. Some knowledge may be expressed in the form of multiple examples consisting of a matrix of attributes that lead to specific conclusions.

9. The main process of inferencing is search.

10. Most knowledge bases are organized as search or decision trees that are graphical, hierarchical structures of nodes representing elements of knowledge interconnected by arcs.

11. Blind search is the process of examining every node in a search tree in an orderly manner until a goal or conclusion is found.

12. Blind search in a large knowledge base leads to combinatorial explosion: the total number of potential outcomes increases exponentially as the number of levels and branches increases. The result may be excessively long search times even with fast processors.

13. Depth-first search looks at successively deeper nodes in a search tree from left to right, backtracking until a goal is found.

14. Breadth-first search looks at all nodes on one level of a tree before going on to the next lower node.

15. Forward-chaining is a search that begins at the root node and works forward or downward in the search tree until a goal is encountered. An initial fact leads to another fact and so on until the conclusion is reached. This is often called a data-driven search.

16. Backward-chaining begins with a goal and works upward in the tree, seeking facts to support the goal. This is called goal-directed search and it is the preferred method of inferencing in most expert systems.

17. Heuristic search refers to techniques that limit or shorten the search, making it more efficient.

Quiz for Chapter 4

1. Knowledge that describes facts and associations is called:
   a. declarative.
   b. definitive.
   c. procedural.
   d. processed.

2. Procedural knowledge describes:
   a. lists of facts.
   b. ways to do things.
   c. methods of representation.
   d. sequences of facts.

3. The most widely used form of knowledge representation in expert systems is:
   a. semantic nets.
   b. frames.
   c. production rules.
   d. search trees.

4. The two main parts of a rule are:
   a. start-finish.
   b. facts-relationships.
   c. nodes-arcs.
   d. premise-conclusion.

5. A number that explains how confident you are of some fact or conclusion is called a:
   a. confidence number.
   b. probability.
   c. priority value.
   d. certainty factor.

6. Which of the following is *not* a way that rules can express inexact knowledge?
   a. Fuzzy logic.
   b. Certainty factor.
   c. Percentage of "rightness."
   d. Probability.

7. A semantic network is a graph showing:
   a. circles and lines.
   b. objects and relationships.
   c. premises and conclusions.
   d. slots and facets.

8. A structure showing detailed stereotyped knowledge about an object with listings of attributes is called a(n):
   a. frame.
   b. semantic network.
   c. hierarchy.
   d. outline.

9. A key feature of frames and semantic networks is:
   a. the ability to deal with uncertainty.
   b. inheritance.
   c. their hierarchical nature.
   d. their simplicity.

10. A knowledge structure that uses examples of attributes and outcomes is a:
    a. frame.
    b. semantic network.
    c. matrix.
    d. decision tree.

11. Another name for the process of search is:
    a. control strategy.
    b. seek and find.
    c. pattern-matching.
    d. interfacing.

12. Most knowledge bases are organized as some form of:
    a. matrix.
    b. network.
    c. rules.
    d. search or decision tree.

13. Search without heuristics is called:
    a. blind search.
    b. hintless.
    c. random search.
    d. pattern-matching.

14. The main disadvantage of search as an inferencing technique is its:
    a. complexity.
    b. non-intuitive nature.
    c. slow speed.
    d. high cost.

15. A data-driven search is called:
    a. forward-chaining.
    b. backward-chaining.
    c. breadth-first.
    d. depth-first.

16. A search that looks at all nodes at one level before going to the next is:
    a. depth-first.
    b. forward-chaining.
    c. backward-chaining.
    d. breadth-first.

17. In depth-first search, a necessary operation is:
    a. heuristic limitation.
    b. backtracking.
    c. backward-chaining.
    d. forward-chaining.

18. Goal-directed search is the same as:
    a. breadth-first.
    b. depth-first.
    c. backward-chaining.
    d. forward-chaining.

19. Most expert systems use:
    a. backward-chaining.
    b. forward-chaining.
    c. a combination of a and b.
    d. sideways-chaining.

20. One type of heuristic in a production system is:
    a. limits on the number of rules.
    b. backward and breadth-first search.
    c. meta rules.
    d. certainty factors.

How Expert Systems Work

So far you've seen what expert systems are and how they can be used. We've explored ways that knowledge is represented in AI software and how search techniques can be applied in order to simulate human thinking. Now, let's put all of these things together and find out how expert systems work.

We know that most AI software consists of two main parts, a knowledge base and an inferencing program. Expert systems certainly have these, but some other elements are required to make them useful. These include a global data base, a user interface, an explanation facility, and a method of entering new knowledge. We'll take a look at each of these major components in this chapter.

Finally, we'll also take an in-depth look at how a rule-based expert system goes about making its decisions and arriving at a conclusion. We'll explore forward- and backward-chaining rule-based expert systems to get a feel for what actually goes on during a consultation.

EXPERT SYSTEM ARCHITECTURE

The main elements of all expert systems are a knowledge base, an inferencing capability, a data base, and a user interface.

Figure 5-1 shows a block diagram of an expert system. These are the main elements of an expert system, although not all expert systems have every subsection. All expert systems have the knowledge base, inference engine, data base, and user interface, but other features will vary from program to program.

Knowledge Base

The knowledge base contains the domain expertise. Most expert systems use production rules and, therefore, the knowledge base is often referred to as a *rule base*. Some expert systems also use semantic networks and frames.

A key feature of an expert system is that the knowledge base is independent of the inference engine that accesses it to solve problems. The knowledge base is formatted in accordance with the

**Figure 5-1.
General Block Diagram
of an Expert System**

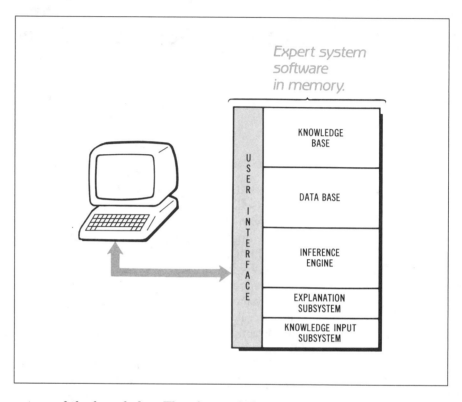

nature of the knowledge. That format is known by the inference
engine so that it can access the IF and THEN portions of the rules
separately as the problem-solving strategy requires.

Since the knowledge base
in rule-based systems is
independent of the
inferencing program,
adding knowledge is fast
and easy.

Since the knowledge base is separate from the algorithmic
programs of the inference engine, should new information become
available or knowledge stored become obsolete, it is relatively easy
to make the necessary changes. All that you have to do is add new
rules, remove old rules, or correct existing rules; reprogramming is
not necessary.

There are no specific guidelines for storing rules in a
knowledge base. In fact, because the inference engine performs a
search of the rule base, the rules may be stored in virtually any
order. Although the rules generally will be stored in some logical
hierarchical sequence, it is not strictly necessary. You could put the
rules in any sequence and the inference engine would find them in
the right order when it goes to solve a problem.

Inference Engine

The inference engine is the algorithm that controls the reasoning process. Also called a "control program" or "rule interpreter," the program works with the input data supplied by the user to search the knowledge base in order to reach a conclusion. Its control strategies implement either forward- or backward-chaining, depth-first or breadth-first search, or a combination of these. The pattern-matching function of the inference engine compares the input data to either the IF or THEN portion of rules in the knowledge base. When a match is found, one portion of the reasoning process is complete. The inference engine continues its search until it provides a solution.

The inference engine is the main controller in an expert system as it implements the search.

The inference engine runs the whole show. Its two basic functions are inference and control. Inference refers to examining the rules and performing the pattern-matching while control refers to the sequence in which rules are examined. The inference engine asks the user for initial input, then it proceeds to search through the rule base looking for rules that match the input. The rule interpreter determines the sequence in which it examines rules, and it asks for additional input information if it cannot make a decision based on the facts it has and the rules available. The inference engine fully automates this process and it is totally invisible when running a consultation.

User Interface

The user interface facilitates user-software communications.

The user interface is a collection of programs that work with the inference engine and the knowledge base to provide a convenient means of two-way communications with the user. The user interface gathers input data in one of two ways. The expert system may ask questions to which the user replies by typing in answers. Or the user interfaces may operate by menus. These offer multiple-choice questions, asking the user to select the correct choice from among several alternatives. This makes data entry fast and simple.

The user interface also comes into play during the inferencing process. Should the rule interpreter find that it cannot reach a decision because it has insufficient information, it notifies the user via the monitor. It may do this by picking up a portion of the rule being tested and reformat it into a question. When the user enters the data asked for, the inference engine can continue its reasoning process.

When the inferencing process is complete an output result is presented on the monitor. Expert systems cannot always reach the right answer, so the screen output may state that no conclusion or only a guess or estimate of the output could be reached. Or the result may be an answer, but with a certainty factor qualifying it.

Simple user interfaces take the verbiage built into the rule base and reformat or resequence it as inputs and outputs. If the rules are written clearly in English, the inputs and outputs should be relatively easy to understand. There is a temptation when creating an expert system to use abbreviations and shorthand notations to minimize the size of rules, but doing so makes the program more difficult to understand.

An expert system may use a natural language front-end or interface. This program uses AI techniques to improve communications between user and expert system. The natural language front-end understands English language inputs and interfaces with the rest of the system to interpret input and convert it to an internally usable form. In the same way, conclusions from the system are reformatted into conversational English. Most expert systems don't use natural language front-ends because they are often as difficult to construct as the entire expert system itself. Generally, only on very large systems can the expense of a natural language front-end be justified.

Data Base

The data base is the expert system's bulletin board for sharing information and status internally.

The data base, sometimes called the global data base or working memory, is the portion of the computer's memory set aside for keeping track of inputs, intermediate conclusions, and outputs. The inference engine uses the data base like a scratch pad to track what's going on in the system.

Initial inputs are stored in the data base. As the rule interpreter sequences through the rules, the conclusions drawn from each of those rules are stored in the data base. The inference engine uses these intermediate conclusions as new inputs to search for new matches. At the end of a run, the data base contains the entire chain of facts that include not only those entered initially but also those that were concluded along the way to the final decision.

Explanation Subsystem

Many expert systems contain a section designed to explain to the user what line of reasoning was used to reach its conclusion. Many users find it difficult to trust the advice of an expert system, not unlike the distrust they might feel for the advice of an unfamiliar human consultant.

Users put more trust in an expert system decision when they can understand its line of reasoning.

One way to solve this problem is to have the system explain how it reached its conclusion. With an explanation subsystem, users can ask "Why?" or "How?" and the system can give an answer. For example, if the system asks for additional input data, the user might wish to ask why. Usually, the system would respond by saying it needs the information to evaluate a particular rule and it might even show which rule it is attempting to satisfy.

Asking how usually causes the system to show the full sequence of rules it examined in order to reach its conclusion. By seeing the logical reasoning process, users can better accept the outcome. Some larger systems annotate the rules and otherwise provide expanded discussion and justification.

The explanation subsystem is also an excellent feature for instructional purposes. Most expert systems quickly provide an answer to a problem, but typically they don't explain their reasoning unless asked. Through solving a number of problems and at the same time asking for an explanation on each, users may begin to understand the reasoning process. With enough practice, users might become experts in their own right.

Users can also use the explanation subsystem for debugging purposes. During development, it can serve as a way to get feedback on rule construction and sequence, enabling users to readily test the system on practical problems.

This capability of explanation by an expert system is often a valuable feature where critical decisions are being made. If users can question the decisions of the system and explore alternatives, they bring their own knowledge to bear on the problem and make the conclusion a thoroughly considered joint decision. For example, a doctor using an expert system to diagnose an illness may want to understand the logical process used by the system and may second-guess its diagnosis.

But not all applications require nor warrant an explanation capability. For example, a fighter pilot using an expert system to help make critical, split-second maneuvering or weapons-choice decisions certainly doesn't have time to question or analyze a decision.

Knowledge Input Subsystem

An expert system needs a way to acquire any additional knowledge it needs to function.

Most expert systems contain a program or set of programs that enables users to add to or modify the rule base. Many expert system domains are dynamic in nature. That is, the knowledge is constantly changing and, therefore, the rule base must be modified to reflect these changes. The knowledge acquisition subsystem provides a convenient means of adding new rules and editing existing rules. While the subsystem is usually a specialized text editor, a standard word processing software package may be used in some systems. In this case, additional rules or rule revisions are keyed in on a word processor and a file created. The knowledge acquisition subsystem reads this information and performs the knowledge base update, acting like a compiler converting the text into the correct format.

Maintaining an expert system is very important. If domain knowledge changes frequently, the expert system begins providing wrong answers if the new knowledge is not added. The knowledge acquisition subsystem provides a fast and convenient way to make these important changes.

EXPERT SYSTEM OPERATION

Now let's see how an expert system actually goes about arriving at a decision. Ours will be a simple rule-based expert system that can perform either forward- or backward-chaining. We'll supply initial inputs and see the actual sequence of rule examinations that the inference engine uses to arrive at a conclusion. Along the way, we'll examine how certainty factors play a role in this conclusion.

Example Knowledge Base

Figure 5-2 shows a seven-rule knowledge base. Instead of using factual statements, we are using symbols—letters of the alphabet—to represent our premise and conclusion statements of heuristic knowledge. In this way, it will be easier to follow the operational sequence. Later, we'll analyze some real expert systems to further explain this process.

Example Data Base

The figure also shows our expert system data base. Note that the initial inputs B and D have been stored there. These facts are the starting point for the inference engine.

Figure 5-2.
Hypothetical Knowledge
Base and Data Base

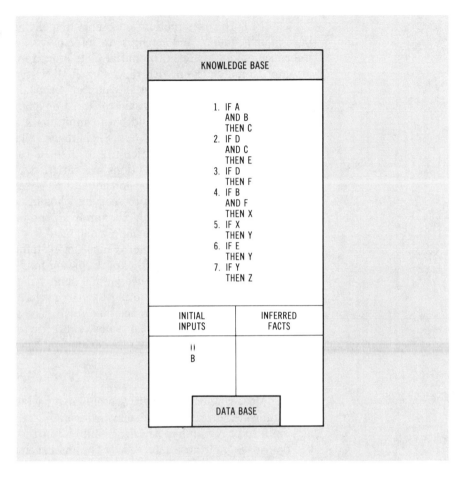

The other part of the data base is allocated to new facts that will be inferred as the inference engine proceeds to analyze the rules. Whenever a rule is satisfied, a new conclusion is drawn and put into the data base. These intermediate conclusions ultimately lead to our final answer.

Inference Engine Operation

The control strategy built into the inference engine determines how the rules in the knowledge base will be examined. Usually, the inference engine, or "rule interpreter" as may be more appropriate in this case, is usually set up to implement either a forward-chaining or a backward-chaining control sequence. We'll take a look at both methods here to be sure you understand how they work.

In both cases the inference engine looks at each rule in a particular sequence and attempts to infer new information. The inference engine will use the initial facts stored in the data base and attempt to match them with the IF or THEN statements in the rules it is examining. We saw in Chapter 4 that if all conditions of a rule are satisfied, the rule is said to fire. For example, in our rule number 1 in *Figure 5-2*, should both conditions A and B be known, then C is inferred and rule 1 *fires*. This means that the designated conclusion is true and the action it expresses is carried out. A rule fires only when all of its conditions are satisfied. When a rule fires, the conclusion drawn is stored in the data base so that it may be used by the inference engine to seek matches in other rules.

Every time a new rule is examined, the inference engine checks the data base to determine what facts it knows and attempts to match them to the new rule. If insufficient information is available to satisfy a rule, the expert system may ask for new inputs. Otherwise, the inference engine simply moves on to the next rule in sequence, again attempting to match what it knows in the data base to the conditions in the rule itself. The inference engine will continue until it runs out of rules and facts. At that point, the expert system usually presents its conclusion.

Backward-Chaining

In backward-chaining, one of the possible outcomes is selected as a hypothesis and the rule base is searched for its proof.

Most rule-based expert systems use backward-chaining in their inferencing process. In backward-chaining, the expert system attempts to prove an hypothesis. Should all of the facts available in the data base and those inferred by the inferencing process prove the hypothesis, then it is assumed to be true and that becomes the output recommendation. All expert systems have stored in them the conclusions that are possible for a given set of problems in the domain. In creating the knowledge base, the expert and the knowledge engineer have to define all possible outcomes. The knowledge base contains a rule that will infer each of those conclusions. The other rules in the knowledge base provide intermediate inferencing steps that will ultimately lead to one of the rules proving the hypothesis. With backward-chaining, the expert system chooses one of these final conclusions as an hypothesis and then attempts to prove it given the input data. Should it not be possible to prove the hypothesis, the inference engine goes on to attempt to prove the next outcome. Sooner or later, the expert system will prove one of the hypotheses and the session will be over.

Refer again to the knowledge base and data base shown in *Figure 5-2*. In this expert system, our hypothesis is Z. For simplicity, we have only one outcome that can be proven. The inference engine begins by looking for Z in the data base to see if it has already been proven. Z is not there. In backward-chaining, the hypothesis is compared to the THEN parts of the rules until a match is achieved. So the inference engine begins its search by looking for rules whose outcome is Z. Only rule 7 matches Z. Now the inference engine needs to prove Y in order for rule 7 to be true and Z to be concluded.

The inference engine looks for Y in the data base. Since it is not there, the inference engine searches for rules that conclude Y. Rules 5 and 6 meet this criteria. The inference engine looks at rule 5 first. To satisfy rule 5, X must be true. X is not in the data base, so the inference engine begins to look for rules that conclude X. Rule 4 is identified but rule 4 requires that both B and F be known if it is to be satisfied.

The inference engine looks in the data base again and finds that condition B is met. B is one of the initial facts we entered. Next, the inference engine looks for F. F is not in the data base so the inference engine begins to look for a rule that concludes F. It discovers rule 3. In order for F to be true, D must be true. The rule interpreter looks for D in the data base and finds it. It too was entered as one of our initial facts.

With this last operation, our hypothesis has been proven. You can see now that rule 3 is satisfied because fact D was initially supplied and, therefore, it concludes F. Rule 4 needs both B and F to conclude X. F is true and B was initially supplied so X is true and rule 4 fires. Since X is now true, rule 5 fires, inferring Y. With Y now known, rule 7 fires, concluding Z, our original hypothesis. Our data base is now shown in *Figure 5-3*.

Assume that the inference engine examines rule 6 instead of rule 5 in attempting to satisfy rule 7. Rules 5 and 6 both conclude Y and either will satisfy the condition in rule 7. If the rule interpreter looks at rule 6, it needs to find E in order to fire. E is not in the data base, so the inference engine looks for a rule that concludes E. It discovers rule 2. In order for rule 2 to fire, facts C and D must be known. The inference engine finds fact D in the data base because it was one of the initial input facts, but it doesn't find C in the data base. It does, however discover rule 1 which infers C. The inference engine then looks for A and B to satisfy rule 1. It finds fact B in the data base but not fact A. A search through the rule base finds that none of the rules conclude A. At this point, the expert system would communicate with the user and ask for

**Figure 5-3.
Hypothetical Knowledge
and Data Base, Inferred
Facts Added**

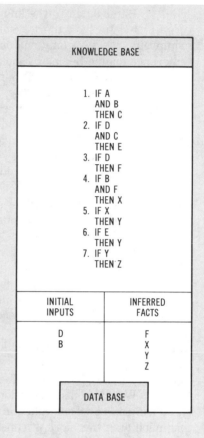

additional input. Should the user be able to supply fact A, then a
new sequence of hypothesis-proving would occur. However, if A is
not known, the system would try another route to prove the
original hypothesis Z. In this case, the system would backtrack and
discover that rule 5 also concludes Y and then take the path
previously described.

There are two key points to remember about backward-
chaining. First, the inference engine attempts to prove one of the
conclusions that it already knows. These conclusions are tested one
after another based on given information. With sufficient input data,
one of the outcomes will be proven.

Second, note that in backward-chaining the inference engine
looks at the THEN part of the rule first and then attempts to prove
the IF portion. It looks in its data base for rules that conclude that
portion of the IF statement. If none of those are possible, it asks

the user to supply the necessary input. Should the necessary input not be available, the inference engine looks for other rules or concludes that the particular hypothesis under test cannot be proven at all. It then moves on to the next hypothesis and each additional hypothesis in sequence until one is proven. Of course, if there is insufficient input data, the system simply cannot supply a conclusion.

Forward-Chaining

In forward-chaining, input facts are matched to rule IF statements until a solution is reached.

If a forward-chaining control sequence is implemented, the inference engine will start with any available facts in the data base and search for those facts in the IF portions of the rules. If the IF part of the rule matches a fact in the data base, the rule is fired. The THEN portion of the rule is said to be true and a new fact is thus inferred and stored in the data base. With this new information, the inference engine moves forward to find this newly inferred fact in the IF part of another rule. This process continues until no further conclusions can be reached. At that point, the expert system has its answer.

To show you how forward-chaining works, we'll begin with the rule base and data base given in *Figure 5-2*. Ultimately, of course, the expert system will conclude that outcome Z is true.

To begin, the inference engine goes to the data base looking for initial facts. It finds that it knows B and D. Therefore, it takes the first one, B, and begins searching rules for IF statements that match. It looks at rule 1 and sees B, but A is also required to fire this rule. A is not in the data base. It moves on to rule 2 and finds no B. Moving on to rule 3, the inference engine finds no B. Rule 4 is examined next. B is found but F, which isn't in the data base, is also required. Rules 5, 6, and 7 are examined without success.

The inference engine backtracks, picking up D from the data base. It looks at rule 1 without a match. Rule 2 contains D but C is not available. Rule 3 contains D and it fires. Thus F is concluded and stored in the data base.

The remaining rules are again tested without success. A conclusion still has not been reached so the inference engine backtracks again. Again it searches for B. The previously described sequence takes place until rule 4 is encountered. The IF statement of rule 4 contains B so a match is found. But rule 4 also requires F to satisfy it. The inference engine looks in the data base for F and finds it there. Recall that F was concluded when rule 3 fired. The conditions for rule 4 are met and, therefore, rule 4 fires, concluding that X is true. X is stored in the data base.

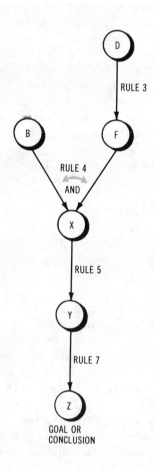

An inference engine
backtracks until it finds
an answer.

The inference engine has used up its initial inputs and now goes on to the new facts that are stored there. These new facts, F and X, were inferred from rules that fired. The rule interpreter first looks for a match to F in the IF portions of rules and finds rule 4, but it has already fired and, therefore, no further action is taken. The inference engine moves on to fact X and begins looking for rules whose IF statements match. It discovers rule 5 which fires and immediately infers Y. Y is added to the data base: The inference engine continues its attempt to match Y to other IF statements in the rule base. It finds rule 7 and, therefore, it fires, concluding Z. Thus the original hypothesis is proven. *Figure 5-4* shows a decision tree whose nodes are the facts and whose arcs represent the rules that fire to conclude those facts.

**Figure 5-4.
Decision Tree Showing
Forward-Chaining Path**

What Have We Learned?

1. Most expert systems comprise the following key parts: knowledge base, inference engine, data base, explanation subsystem, and knowledge input subsystem.

2. Production rules usually make up the knowledge base, but frames or other knowledge structures may also be used.

3. The data base is the working memory area where the current status of the system is stored.

4. The inference engine implements either a forward- or backward-chaining control strategy.

5. The user interface facilitates communications between the software and the user.

6. A knowledge input (acquisition) subsystem provides a convenient means of entering new rules or making modifications to the rule base.

7. The explanation subsystem tells the user the "line of reasoning" followed by the inference engine in reaching its final conclusion. This helps the user understand and accept the decision.

8. In forward-chaining, the inference engine compares facts in the data base to IF statements.

9. In backward-chaining, the inference engine compares the facts in the data base to THEN statements.

Quiz for Chapter 5

1. The operation of the expert system is controlled by the:
   a. knowledge base.
   b. inference engine.
   c. user interface.
   d. user.

2. Most expert systems use which type of knowledge representation?
   a. Production rules.
   b. Frames.
   c. Semantic networks.
   d. Examples.

3. What feature of an expert system makes it easy to revise and add to a knowledge base?
   a. Forward-chaining.
   a. Backward-chaining.
   c. Explanation subsystem.
   d. Knowledge base independent of the inference engine.

4. A user communicates with the expert system through the:
   a. computer I/O ports.
   b. explanation subsystem.
   c. user interface.
   d. inference engine.

5. The part of the expert system that serves as a kind of status board is the:
   a. knowledge base.
   b. inference engine.
   c. data base.
   d. explanation subsystem.

6. To modify the knowledge base, a user must communicate through the:
   a. explanation subsystem.
   b. knowledge input subsystem.
   c. data base.
   d. knowledge base.

7. In the rule
   IF   X
   AND   Y
   THEN   Z
   the inference engine would see which of the following if forward-chaining was used?
   a. X and Y.
   b. Z.
   c. X and Z.
   d. Y and Z.

8. Which inferencing method tries to verify an hypothesis?
   a. Forward-chaining.
   b. Depth-first search.
   c. Breadth-first search.
   d. Backward-chaining.

9. If an inference engine cannot find an answer after one pass through the rule base, it:
   a. stops.
   b. backtracks.
   c. goes into an endless loop.
   d. switches from forward- to backward-chaining or vice versa.

10. To start the search, the inference engine must be:
    a. told which rules to test.
    b. told which rules to start on.
    c. set to forward- or backward-chaining.
    d. given some initial facts.

Expert System Development Tools

Expert systems are software, and most of the conventional software development techniques can be used to create them. Expert systems can be developed using any of the standard programming languages on virtually any computer. There are special software packages, however, that greatly facilitate the creation of expert systems and other artificial intelligence software. These include AI programming languages as well as programs designed to help create expert systems without programming. These software development tools greatly expedite the development process. This is particularly true of *shells*, a special class of expert system development program.

In this chapter we introduce the software tools to create expert system packages, including the main AI programming languages, LISP and Prolog. For the greater part of the chapter, however, we'll focus on expert system shells.

SPECTRUM OF DEVELOPMENT TOOLS

A *development tool* is a program or collection of programs that facilitates the creation of other software. There are all kinds of tools—general tools for generic software development, AI tools, and expert system tools. A spectrum of such tools is shown in *Figure 6-1*. To the left are the generic tools, mostly conventional languages. In the center are the AI languages and the shells are on the right. Note the ease of use and development time indicators. The languages are harder to use, the shells are the easiest to use. It takes longer to create an expert system with a standard language than with a shell. We'll discuss these tools in the order shown in *Figure 6-1*.

**Figure 6-1.
Spectrum of Expert
System Development
Tools**

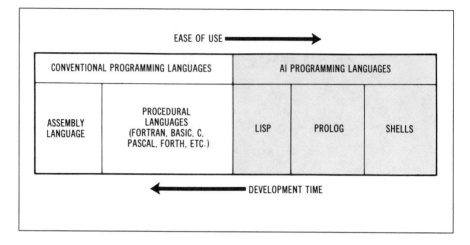

CONVENTIONAL PROGRAMMING LANGUAGES

You can program AI in any language.

Expert systems have been created using almost every major programming language, including FORTRAN, BASIC, Pascal, Forth, C, and assembly language. If you are a competent programmer, experienced in one of these languages, your best choice may be to use that language to create an expert system. Learning a new language is time consuming and difficult, so development can be facilitated by programming in the language with which you are most familiar.

C is the most popular development language today.

When LISP or Prolog isn't used, most AI programming is done in one of the structured languages such as Pascal or C. Modula-2 and Ada have also been used. Forth, because it is extensible and easily implements recursive functions, is also used to create expert systems. However, the trend for most AI development is to the use of the C programming language, which is extremely flexible and produces fast code.

The major need in creating expert systems and AI software is computing speed. Search and pattern-matching processes are inherently slow and development methods should take into consideration the impact of the programming language on them. For example, BASIC interpreters generally should not be used unless the program is relatively small. BASIC and interpreters are both inherently slow and, in most cases, not suitable for large systems. FORTRAN is also somewhat slow. Pascal, Forth, and C usually generate faster code. If the ultimate in speed is necessary, the choice should be assembly language. For the greatest efficiency in using the machine, nothing can compare with assembly language; with it, you can create compact, very high-speed code for such programs as real-time expert systems.

When programming in a conventional language, every element of the expert system must be created from scratch. This is also true with LISP, but not with Prolog, as we will see. A format for the knowledge base must be devised. The control strategies for the inference engine must be determined and programmed. The data base, user interface, and other subprograms must be created. For even a skilled programmer, this represents a challenging project, but don't despair. You have several alternatives to conventional languages when creating an expert system.

AI PROGRAMMING LANGUAGES

A number of programming languages have been created to deal specifically with AI applications. The most popular AI languages are LISP and Prolog. A less popular, but important language is Smalltalk. With these, the software development process is eased, and expert systems and other AI software can be created more readily than with conventional programming languages. In this section, we'll concentrate on LISP, Prolog, and Smalltalk.

LISP Programming

LISP is the oldest and still the most useful AI language.

LISP is by far the most widely used AI programming language. Programmers prefer it because of its flexibility in creating AI programs. It is relatively easy to learn and LISP interpreters and compilers are available for practically every computer.

LISP is so important that special computers, called "LISP machines," have been created to implement the language. Most serious AI programming is done in LISP. While we don't have space to introduce the language in depth, we will survey its basic features and capabilities.

LISP was developed in the 1950s by John McCarthy at MIT. Next to FORTRAN, it is the oldest high-level computer language. It became commercially available in the early 1960s. Over the years, LISP has been modified and redefined many times; there are many "dialects" of LISP in use. A list of dialects is given in *Table 6 1*. The most widely used versions of LISP are MacLISP, developed at MIT; InterLISP; and portable standard LISP. More recently, however, a generic version called Common LISP has become popular. Common LISP is the result of efforts to standardize to a version of LISP that everyone can use. This is highly desirable as it enables programs to be transferred from one computer to another without reprogramming. Currently, most LISP programs are not portable between machines because of the wide variations in the different dialects.

Table 6-1.
Dialects of LISP

Dialect	Publisher
BYSO LISP	Levien Instrument
Common LISP	Gold Hill Computers
DG Common LISP	Data General
ExperLISP	ExperTelligence
FranzLISP	Franz, Inc.
InterLISP-D	Xerox
IQLISP	Integral Quality
ISI-INTERLISP	Digital Equipment Corp.
Le-LISP	CRIL
LISP/VM	IBM
LISP/80	Software Toolworks
LISP/88	Norell Data Systems
MacLISP	MIT (Franz, Zeta)
Microsoft LISP	Microsoft Corp.
muLISP	Microoft Corp., The Coft Warehouse
P-LISP	Gnosis, Inc.
PC-LISP	IOTC, Inc.
PC Scheme LISP	Texas Instruments
Portable Standard LISP	University of Utah
TLC-LISP 86	The Lisp Co.
TransLISP	Solution Systems
UNXLISP	Cybermetrics
UNXLISP-86	Automata Design Associates
UO-LISP	Northwest Computer Algorithms
VAXLISP	Digital Equipment Corp.
WaltzLISP	Pro Code International
XLISP	PC/Blue Users Group
ZetaLISP	LMI, Symbolics, Xerox

Most LISPs are interpreters that must be co-resident with the applications program, but some LISPs may also be compiled.

The LISP language is available as interpreters and compilers. The majority of LISPs are interpreters, making them highly interactive for program development. An interpreter is a program stored in memory that interprets programs written in that language. The program to be executed, also stored in memory, is examined line-by-line and command-by-command by the interpreter. As each line of code is deciphered, it is executed. Subroutines in the interpreter cause the desired operation to occur in the correct sequence. Interpreters execute relatively slowly, but programs can be written quickly and tested without the major manipulations required by compilers.

A compiler is a translation program that converts the high-level-language source program into a machine-language object program that can be executed by the computer. The programmer uses an editor to write the code in the desired language. This source program is fed to the compiler, which translates it into the binary computer instructions compatible with the host computer. The compiler output is the object program, which is usually stored on disk and then loaded into memory for execution.

A compiler executes many times faster than the same program run by an interpreter. In addition, the compiler, unlike the interpreter, does not have to be co-resident in RAM to execute the program. During program development, however, numerous editing changes and recompiling are necessary to work out the bugs and get the program running.

And don't forget, LISP is available as a special computer. The language itself is preprogrammed into the hardware. Typically, special microcodes stored in ROM implement the main features of LISP. A 36- or 40-bit word CPU whose architecture is optimized for this language is used. For serious LISP development efforts, LISP machines are recommended despite their high cost compared with conventional computers.

List Fundamentals

LISP is an acronym for LISt Processing. It is a symbolic programming language that represents and manipulates information stored as *lists*, also called *expressions*. Almost anything can be represented by items in a list and by grouping and sequencing them appropriately. LISP also provides a wide range of methods by which to manipulate lists. While the bulk of LISP operations are symbolic, LISP can also perform basic arithmetic operations.

Atoms

An atom is the basic data element in LISP. An atom may be a number, a word, or an alphanumeric combination. These symbols can represent data or any person, place, or thing. Here are some examples of LISP atoms:

TRAIN   −17

Sally   0.0833

G2   transportation__mode

LISP compilers create faster programs and the compiler does not have to be co-resident.

LISP machines have a special CPU in which LISP has been embedded in microcode.

A list is a simple but flexible vehicle by which knowledge can be represented.

Atoms are the individual elements of a list.

Spaces aren't allowed in an atom. Multiple-word atoms may be implemented by separating the words or segments by a hyphen or underline symbol. Atoms combining letters and numbers are allowed but the letters must occur first. For example, 300E is not allowed.

Lists

Listed here are several examples of sequences of atoms that form a list. A list is defined by parentheses and individual items in the list are separated by spaces. Note that a list of items usually will have a characteristic in common.

(CAR SAILBOAT TRAIN AIRPLANE SNOWMOBILE)

(2000 6000 300 9000 5000)

(Joan Bud Ann John Sally)

It is also possible to make up large lists from smaller lists.

((A B C D)(E F G H)(I J K))

(((W X)(Y Z))(T U V))

Lists within lists are said to be nested. When working with lists, you must keep track of the parentheses, which gets tricky when multiple lists are nested. Some LISP versions do this for you automatically.

If you consider it, lists are a flexible way to structure information. Hierarchies and outlines are particularly easy to reduce to list format. Any form of knowledge representation is easily implemented with lists. *Figure 6-2* shows how a list can represent a search or decision tree.

Procedures

The basic operation in LISP is the manipulation of lists using LISP procedures or functions. A procedure is an operation, usually defined by a word or by an atom, that causes a list to be manipulated. The LISP interpreter or compiler reads the first element in the list as a procedure. It evaluates the procedure and prints out the result. LISP programs are sequences of procedures that operate one after another on lists until the desired processing has been accomplished. The LISP interpreter or compiler will repeat this read-evaluate-manipulate-print cycle again and again until the program is complete.

Figure 6-2.
List Representing a
Search or Decision Tree

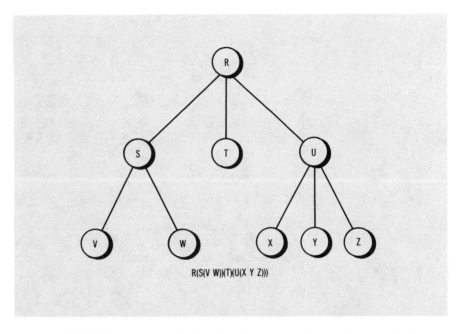

R(S(V W))(T)(U(X Y Z)))

Procedures operate on
lists to perform some
useful job.

All LISPs are provided with a basic set of procedures called primitives. These predefined procedures permit you to perform a variety of arithmetic and decision-making operations. You construct LISP programs by putting these primitives in the desired order. Additionally, a most important feature about LISP is that you can create your own procedures and functions. Using the predefined primitives, you can assemble and name procedures that will perform the unique operations required by your problem.

Primitives

LISP primitives perform basic mathematical operations. Not known for its calculating power, LISP can calculate only on a limited scale: addition, subtraction, multiplication, and division. Often special operations, such as square root, can also be performed.

Listed here are examples of how to perform mathematical operations in LISP.

addition	[+ 8 6]
	14
subtraction	[− 12 5]
	7

multiplication   [* 9 −3]
                   −27
     division   [/ 100 4]
                    25

Note that each mathematical operation is written as a list. A symbol such as the plus sign designates the operation to be performed. This symbol may be replaced by a word naming the procedure:

[PLUS 7 4]
11

The remaining elements in the list are those items to be operated on. In each of these examples, the first line indicates the list to be processed and the second line indicates the result obtained when LISP evaluates the procedure and prints out the results. Only two quantities may be used in a computation.

Another kind of LISP primitive is the predicate. Predicates are procedures that answer questions about an argument in a list and provide a true or false answer. *Table 6-2* shows some of the more common predicates used in LISP and examples of their use.

Predicates make true-false decisions based on expressions.

**Table 6-2.
Common LISP
Predicates**

UMBERP	*Tells if an atom is a number or a symbol.*
	NUMBERP 85)
	T
	(NUMBERP GOLD)
	NIL
ATOMP	*Tells if an expression is an atom.*
	(ATOMP H8)
	T
	(ATOMP GOLD SILVER PLATINUM)
	NIL
LISTP	*Tells if an expression is a list.*
	(LISTP GOLD SILVER PLATINUM)
	T
	(LISTP PC/2)
	NIL
ZEROP	*Tells if a number is zero.*
	(ZEROP 0)
	T
	(ZEROP −8)
	NIL

**Table 6-2
Cont.**

ODDP	*Tells if a number is odd.* (ODDP 13) T (ODDP 14) NIL
EVENP	*Tells if a number is even.* (EVENP 88) T (EVENP 23) NIL
EQUAL	*Compares two expressions to see if they are the same.* (EQUAL 12 12) T (EQUAL GT GT) T (EQUAL (T U V)(T U W)) NIL
GREATERP	*Tells if the first number is greater than the second.* (GREATERP 100 99) T (GREATERP 49 50) NIL
LESSP	*Tells if the first number is less than the second number.* (LESSP 18 36) T (LESSP 45 19) NIL

Note in the examples that each expression begins with the name of the predicate. The remaining items in the list will be evaluated. There are only two outputs that LISP will return upon evaluating the arguments of the expression, true, or T, or false, designated by the expression NIL. NIL is also used to refer to an empty list. An empty list contains no atoms and is expressed by parentheses: ().

Other primitives supplied in LISP are used primarily for building and dissecting lists. These primitives let you search through, examine, rearrange, and perform other operations on the elements in a list. *Table 6-3* lists some of the more common primitives for assembling and disassembling lists.

Table 6-3.
Useful LISP Predicates
for Working on Lists

CAR	Extracts and returns the first element of a list.
CDR	Returns all elements or atoms of a list except the first.
APPEND	Adds two lists together, end-to-end, forming one list.
CONS	Adds an element to the front of a list.

Here are several examples of how to use these primitives. CAR is used to pick out the first element in a list. The CDR function returns all of the items in the list except for the first. With these two primitives, you can manipulate lists to pick out any element.

```
[CAR '[TOM JIM BOB BILL]]
TOM
[CDR '[TOM JIM BOB BILL]]
[JIM BOB BILL]
```

In the next example, the given function returns the third item in a list.

```
[CAR [CDR [CDR '[TOM JIM BOB BILL]]]]
BOB
```

LISP works from the inside out. The inside CDR first produces (JIM BOB BILL). The second CDR produces (BOB BILL). Finally, the CAR picks up the first element, BOB.

The single quotation mark in all of these expressions tells LISP which part of the expression to evaluate and which part to ignore. This single quote separates the procedure name from the list that is to be evaluated. This symbol helps LISP separate the procedure name from the list to be operated upon.

APPEND lets you combine lists to form larger lists. CONS allows you to build new lists from scratch or to modify existing lists. The examples given are self-explanatory.

```
[APPEND ' [TOM JIM BOB BILL][TED SAM]]
[TOM JIM BOB BILL TED SAM]
[CONS ' HERB ' [TOM JIM BOB BILL]]
[HERB TOM JIM BOB BILL]
```

The SETQ primitive is used to assign values to variable names.

To set K = 39

[SETQ K 39]

To set L = 48

[SETQ L 48]

Creating New Procedures

Programming in LISP primarily entails creating new procedures that perform the work to be done.

As we saw earlier, the most important feature of LISP is that it is extensible. That means you can create special procedures to do exactly the kinds of processing your problem requires. We create a new procedure by using DEFUN, which stands for DEfine FUNction. When DEFUN appears as the first element in a list, LISP accepts the procedure and uses it as if it were one of the readily available primitives. Let's look at an example.

Suppose we wish to create a procedure to compute the age of a person in the year 1990. Their birth date is Y. Our procedure would look like this:

[DEFUN AGE [Y][- 1990 Y]]

The word following DEFUN becomes the name of the new procedure. Normally you will use a one-word atom describing what kind of operation the procedure will perform. This enables you to remember it easily and enables others examining the program to determine more easily what is happening. The remainder of the expression is made up of variables and primitives that perform the specific operation desired. To use the new procedure, call it along with a value for Y.

[AGE 1944]
46

Decisions and Repetitions

An important procedure in LISP is the COND primitive which is used for decision-making. COND stands for conditional. The COND expression consists of one or more lists called "clauses." Clauses contain a condition to be met and a corresponding action to take place when the condition is met. The action part is usually something to be evaluated. Here's an example:

[COND [condition, action]]
[COND [LESSP X TARGET] ' OK]

If X is less than TARGET, the expression OK is returned.

There are primitives within LISP that enable you to perform *iteration*, the process of repeating an operation again and again. In other programming languages, this is done by constructing a program loop. A sequence of instructions is executed and then a condition is tested for. The program loops back and repeats the sequence until the desired condition is detected. LISP can perform iterative operations with such primitives as PROG and DO, but most repetitive operations in LISP are taken care of by *recursion*.

With recursion, a procedure calls itself.

Recursion is an operation in which a procedure is implemented by referring to the procedure itself. Recursion is easy to implement in LISP and widely used in defining new functions.

Production Rules

Production rules are easy to write with LISP.

Expert systems can be easily implemented with LISP. Because of the flexibility of LISP's structure, almost any knowledge representation scheme can be handled. For example, production rules can be written in a list format.

[RULE [WEEKEND [IF [RAIN] THEN [NOT BEACH]]]]

This rule says we won't go to the beach this weekend if it rains. In our example, the rule name is WEEKEND. (We could have appended a number to RULE.) RAIN is the IF condition and NOT BEACH is the THEN action.

Other LISP Characteristics

Property lists let you implement knowledge structures such as frames and semantic nets.

LISP can also set up and maintain special property lists. The items in these lists are referred to as properties and you can assign each value. Property lists can be used to form a variety of knowledge bases.

Search and pattern-matching techniques are also easily implemented in LISP. Using the various primitives, you can create pattern-matching functions and search procedures to match your problem exactly. For example, you can use the EQUAL predicate to compare expressions.

LISP is powerful, flexible, and widely used; it is considered to be "the" AI language. If you plan to do a lot of work in the field of AI, LISP is worth learning. Purchase one of the inexpensive LISP interpreters for your personal computer and within a short time, you should have a good operating knowledge of this powerful language.

PROLOG

Prolog is the AI language of choice in Europe and Japan.

Another programming language that is rapidly gaining acceptance in the AI community is Prolog. It was created during the 1970s in France and has been widely used throughout Europe for AI programming. In fact, Prolog may be more widely used in Europe for AI than LISP. Prolog has also been adopted by the Japanese as the primary language for creating their Fifth Generation AI-based computer systems, which are expected to be available in the 1990s.

Procedural vs. Declarative Languages

Although Prolog and LISP are both AI programming languages, they are completely different from one another. LISP is a *procedural* programming language, much like other standard programming languages. In a procedural language instructions, statements, and commands are listed step-by-step to solve a particular algorithm. Each of these languages has its own syntax for describing the steps. All programming languages, including LISP but not Prolog, are procedural in this way.

Prolog is a *declarative* language. In creating a Prolog program, you don't list individual processing steps. Rather, you give the computer a set of facts and rules describing objects and their relationships. These facts and rules are expressed as clauses that make statements that are true. In this way, Prolog is an implementation of the procedures used in predicate calculus, a type of logic programming used to solve mathematical and symbolic problems. Given certain facts and how to use them, Prolog enables you to draw conclusions and make inferences. Prolog, in fact, means *Programming in logic*.

Procedural languages are used to solve algorithms. Declarative languages let the computer determine how to solve the problem.

How Prolog Works

You give Prolog the facts and rules which, in effect, constitute the knowledge base Prolog uses to solve problems. Prolog has a built-in inference engine that performs search and pattern-matching. In fact, most Prologs implement backward-chaining.

To use Prolog, you ask questions regarding the facts and rules you supplied earlier. Assuming you provided sufficient information, the inference engine searches the knowledge base and provides answers to your questions. As you can see, you don't have to tell Prolog how to solve the problem. Its built-in inference engine does this for you. All you need to do is supply the necessary knowledge in the proper format.

The structure and operation of Prolog is ideal for expert systems.

Prolog is usable for many artificial intelligence applications, such as natural language processing, but, because of its unique structure, it is ideal for implementing expert systems. You can create an expert system without having to develop the subroutines for search, pattern-matching, user interface, and so on. The main benefit of Prolog is that it can be used by programmers and even non-programmers to create expert systems, often making the software development faster and less expensive.

Like LISP, Prolog is available in a number of dialects. There is no particular standard and it's unlikely one will be produced any time soon. One of the more popular versions of Prolog is described in *Programming in Prolog* (Springer-Verlag, 1984) by Clocksin and Mellish of the University of Edinburgh (Scotland).

Prolog is available as either an interpreter or compiler. Interpreter versions are more widely available, and they make programming fast and easy because they are interactive. Prolog compilers, however, provide shorter, faster code for more efficient operation. Prolog is available for most mainframes, minicomputers, and personal computers.

Programming in Prolog

Programming in Prolog is basically a two-step process. First, you write facts that define the objects of your knowledge base by assigning attributes to the objects. Second, you create rules that define relationships between the objects.

Once your knowledge base is formed, using the system is easy. All you have to do is ask questions about the objects in the knowledge base. You may ask about relationships or attributes. This enables you to solve problems by drawing conclusions from the knowledge available.

Entering Facts

Facts are stated in clauses with a predicate that describes the relationship between arguments.

The basic element in Prolog is a clause about an object or objects and a relationship. Here are some typical Prolog expressions:

```
city__in[houston,texas]
city__in[charlottesville,virginia]
city__in[lansing,michigan]
```

The first word ("city__in") is called the predicate, and it states a relationship between two arguments given in parentheses. To convert this statement into an English language expression, all you have to do is simply insert the predicate between the two arguments and read the result.

You may also write a Prolog statement with only one argument. This kind of statement is frequently used to assign attributes to objects.

```
fat [horace]
skinny [doris]
gray [sky]
```

A number of such statements constitutes your knowledge base. To use it, you type in a question using the predicate-argument format preceded or followed by a question mark. The exact format is determined by the Prolog language you are using, so be sure to check your reference manual before writing software.

The Prolog interpreter takes the question and the inference engine searches the knowledge base. It does a standard pattern-matching routine that attempts to match up the predicates in your question with the predicates in the various statements of the knowledge base. Using backward-chaining, it finds all appropriate matches and outputs an answer. The answer is usually a simple yes or no. Let's look at some examples using the statements given before as the knowledge base.

We can ask, "Is Charlottesville a city in Virginia?" You type in:

```
city__in [charlottesville,virginia]?
```

The computer responds:

```
YES
```

You can also ask:

```
city__in [norfolk,virginia]?
NO
```

Even though Norfolk is a city in Virginia, the computer answers no because it does not know this fact. You get a "no" to unknowns.

Try asking:

```
fat [doris]?
NO
```

That's true.

```
skinny [doris]?
YES
```

You can also use variables in Prolog statements. A variable is either a capital letter or a word that begins with a capital. This easily distinguishes them from all of the predicates and arguments in other Prolog statements, which are always lowercase. With variables, you can ask more sophisticated questions. When you use a variable, the inference engine searches the data base seeking to match up the variable to some known argument. Here's an example:

```
city__in [X,virginia]?
charlottesville
fat [Z]?
horace
```

Rules

Rules in Prolog are just like production rules.

In addition to creating statements of facts for the knowledge base, you can also create rules. These rules typically have an IF-THEN format much like production rules, although they are written in a different way. Take this simple production rule:

```
IF     Rockville is a city in Montgomery
AND    Montgomery is a county in Maryland
THEN   Rockville is a city in Maryland
```

This rule can also be expressed:

```
city__in [rockville maryland]:-
city__in [rockville montgomery],
city__in [montgomery maryland]
```

The primary difference is that the THEN portion of the rule is stated first, followed by the special symbol that looks like a colon followed by a dash. This special symbol means IF. The conditions or premises of the rule are listed after that. The comma separating the second and third clauses means *and*.

The mixture of facts and rules combine to form a powerful and capable knowledge base. Given sufficient information, Prolog can solve complex logical problems as long as you ask the correct questions. For example, the rule above fires if you ask:

```
city__in [rockville maryland]?
YES
```

Most Prologs also contain procedural statements and instructions that can be used to build more conventional software. The knowledge base and inference engine are inherent in Prolog while the procedural parts of the language are easier to use in constructing I/O routines for the user interface and other standard operations.

OTHER AI LANGUAGES

Many special AI
languages have been
created in research labs
and universities.

LISP is by far the most widely used AI programming
language. However, the use of Prolog is greatly increasing. No
doubt more than 80 percent of AI programming efforts are in one of
these two languages. The remaining 20 percent includes
conventional languages as well as a variety of other AI languages.

Over the years, many special languages have been created
for use in artificial intelligence work. Most of these come out of
universities and research labs, and few were successful commercial
products. *Table 6-4* lists some of the better-known languages of this
type. In the AI community, Smalltalk and programs like it, such as
Loops and Flavors, are most often used.

**Table 6-4.
Special AI Languages**

Program	Development
CONNIVER	Improved and enhanced version of PLANNER
FLAVORS	Object-based language like LOOPS but for use on the Symbolics and LMI LISP machines
FRL	Frame-based language
KRL	Frame-based language developed by Stanford and Xerox
LOGLISP	Combination of LISP and Prolog
LOGO	Derivative of LISP used in teaching computers and programming
LOOPS	Programming language featuring rules, objects, and logic implemented in Xerox's InterLISP
OPS5	Rule-based language developed at Carnegie-Mellon University. Includes procedural syntax as well as a forward-chaining inference engine
PLANNER	Prolog-like language written on top of LISP
POPLOG	Mix of LISP, Prolog, and POP-11. A deduction/theorem prover language
SAIL	Prolog-like language built on top of Algol
Smalltalk	Object-based language developed at Xerox. A subset of LOOPS

Smalltalk and other
object-based languages
are gaining popularity in
AI work.

Smalltalk is an object-based language developed at Xerox's
Palo Alto Research Center. An object is defined as an element of
data that can be either symbolic or numeric. The object also
contains a description of the operations that can be performed on it.
As a result, objects are really a combination of declarative and
procedural knowledge.

Objects are further classified into one or more categories referred to as "acquaintances." The objects in an acquaintance can inherit characteristics of other objects in the acquaintance.

To program in Smalltalk, you send messages between objects. A message is usually a word describing a type of manipulation that can be performed on the object. Objects know what they can do and, therefore, recognize a valid message when received. The object implements the manipulation and generates a response.

Object-based languages are suitable for many AI applications including expert systems. There is growing interest in Smalltalk as well as other object-based languages.

EXPERT SYSTEM SHELLS

Most expert systems are developed with shells, not languages.

An expert system shell is a collection of programs that enables you to create an expert system without using a programming language. Because no programming expertise is required to use a shell, these development tools have been responsible for fostering the development and use of expert systems. While shells cannot eliminate all the difficulties of creating an expert system, they do eliminate the programming that prevents many from considering this form of software.

Take the domain knowledge out of an expert system and you have a shell.

An expert system shell, or "generator" as it is sometimes called, is a completely implemented expert system without a knowledge base. The shell contains an inference engine, user interface, and an explanation facility, and it usually has a convenient form for entering the knowledge base. Most shells use production rules and have a unique knowledge base organization and format.

Shells are derived from early expert system research and development. In the early expert system MYCIN, the inference engine and other programs were separate from the knowledge base, so the medical knowledge base could be removed and a knowledge base on another subject substituted. Among other shells are another version of MYCIN, known as essential or empty MYCIN (EMYCIN); the KAS development tool, derived from PROSPECTOR; and EXPERT, derived from CASNET, an expert system for diagnosis and treatment of glaucoma.

Expert system shells are available for a wide range of computers. Dozens of shells are available for personal computers, principally the IBM PC. Expert system shells are also available for the DEC VAX minicomputer and other minicomputers and mainframes. Many shells have also been developed for the more popular LISP machines, such as those from LMI, Symbolics, Texas Instruments, and Xerox.

Shells can greatly simplify and speed development of expert systems. Given that no complex programming is required, they may lower costs as well. In Chapter 7 we'll concentrate on developing an expert system with a shell. But for now, we'll introduce the various types of shell, describe their capabilities and limitations, and discuss some of the commercial products available.

Types of Shells

Two basic types of shell are available: rule-based and induction. Hybrids are also available. Some rule-based shells also permit the creation of frames or semantic networks. Some induction shells allow the creation of rules.

Rule-Based Shells

Rule-based shells are most common.

A rule-based shell uses production rules for representing knowledge. Each shell has its own guidelines for typing a rule into the knowledge base. Although the variations are minor, it is essential that the correct format be used for each shell.

When acquiring knowledge from the expert, keep in mind that it must be representable as rules.

To create an expert system, you extract the knowledge from the expert with a process known as knowledge engineering. We will discuss that in more detail in the next chapter. The knowledge is analyzed, organized, and codified. From this organization of knowledge, production rules are written. The method of knowledge representation guides the knowledge engineering process, so knowing that the expert's knowledge must be translated into IF-THEN rules makes it somewhat easier to obtain that knowledge.

The rules are typed in the desired format by using an editor or word processing program. Some shells require that an ASCII file of the rules in the desired format be created separately. The expert system shell reads the file to use it in the inferencing process. Some expert systems have a built-in rule editor, a simplified word processing program that lets you build and edit a file in the desired format. Some systems compile the ASCII file into the correct format for the inference engine.

Once the rules are entered, the program may be tested. The inference engine asks questions, searches the knowledge base, and eventually produces a solution.

Rule-based shells are available in a variety of sizes and shapes for mainframes, minicomputers, and personal computers. Their characteristics, features, and specifications vary widely. *Tables 6-5* and *6-6* list available shells.

**Table 6-5.
Expert System
Development Tools for
Personal Computers**

Program	Publisher	Computer	Type
ADVISOR	Ultimate Media	Apple II, Commodore 64	Rules
AL/X	Univ. of Edinburgh, Scotland	Apple II	Rules
CxPERT	Software Plus	IBM PC	Frames, Rules
DAISY	Lithp Systems	IBM PC	Rules, Frames, Semantic Nets
ESI	Abacus Programming Corp.	IBM PC	Rules
ES/P Advisor	Expert Systems Int'l	IBM PC	Rules
Expert Ease	Expert Systems Int'l & Human Edge Software, Inc.	IBM PC	Induction
Expert Edge	Human Edge Software, Inc.	IBM PC	Rules
Expert-2	Mountain View Press, Inc.	IBM PC	Rules
Expert One	Softsync Inc.	IBM PC	Induction
ExperOPS5	ExperTelligence	Apple MacIntosh	Rules
Expert System	Potomac Pacific Engineering	IBM PC	Rules
Expert Systems Toolkit (EST)	Mind Path Technologies, Inc.	IBM PC	Rules
EXSYS	Exsys, Inc.	IBM PC	Rules
1st Class	Programs in Motion, Inc.	IBM PC	Rules or Induction
FLOPS 1.2	Kemp-Carraway Heart Institute	IBM PC	Rules, Fuzzy logic
GURU	Micro Data Base Systems, Inc.	IBM PC	Rules

**Table 6-5
Cont.**

Program	Publisher	Computer	Type
INSIGHT	Level 5 Research	IBM PC	Rules
Intelligence/ Compiler 1.0a	Intelligence Ware Inc.	IBM PC	Rules
KDS	KDS Corp.	IBM PC	Induction
KES II	Software A&E, Inc.	IBM PC	Rules
KNOWOL	Intelligent Machine Co.	IBM PC	Rules
M.1	Teknowledge Inc.	IBM PC	Rules
Methods	Digitalk	IBM PC	Character-Based
Micro Expert	McGraw-Hill	IBM PC	Rules
Micro-PS	Ashton-Tate	IBM PC	Rules
NEXPERT	Neuron Data Inc.	IBM PC/AT, Apple MacIntosh	Rules
OPS5+	Artelligence, Inc.	IBM PC, Apple MacIntosh	Rules
OPS/83	Production Systems Technologies Inc.	IBM PC	Rules
Personal Consultant (Plus and Easy)	Texas Instruments	IBM PC, TI PC	Rules
RuleMaster	Radian Corp.	IBM PC	Induction
SeRIES	SRI International	IBM PC	Rules
Shells	ExpertTelligence	IBM PC	Rules
TIMM	General Research Corp.	IBM PC	Induction
TOPSI	Dynamic Master Systems Inc.	IBM PC, CP/M Machines	Rules
Turbo Expert	Thinking Software Inc.	IBM PC	Rules
VP-Expert	Paperback Software Inc.	IBM PC	Rules or Induction
XSYS	California Intelligence	IBM PC	Rules

Table 6-6.
Expert System
Development Tools for
Microcomputers,
Mainframes, LISP
Machines

Program	Vendor	Computer	Type
ADS	Aion Corp.	IBM/MVS/VM	Rules
Contessa	Prophecy Development Corp.	TI Explorer	Special procedural language
DUCK	Smart Systems Technology	DEC VAX, Symbolics, Sun, IBM	Predicate calculus
ESE/MVS	IBM	IBM/MVS	Rules
HPRL	Hewlett-Packard Co.	HP, DEC VAX	Frames
IKE	LMI	LMI	Rules
KEE	Intellicorp	Xerox, Symbolics, LMI	Rules, Frames
KES	Software A&E Inc.	TI, Symbolics	Rules
Knowledge	Carnegie Group	LMI, DEC VAX	Rules
LOOPS	Xerox	Xerox	Rules (also a language)
NEXPERT	Newcon Data	DEC VAX	Rules
OPS/83	Production Systems Technologies Inc.	DEC VAX, AT&T, Apollo, Tektronix	Rules
PICON	LMI	LMI	Rules
REVEAL	McDonnell Douglass	DEC VAX	Logic and a programming language
RuleMaster	Radian Corp.	DEC VAX, TI	Induction
S.1	Teknowledge Inc.	DEC VAX, Symbolics	Rules
SRL+	The Carnegie Group Inc.	DEC VAX	Rules
TIMM	General Research Corp.	IBM, Amdahl, DEC VAX, Prime	Induction
TWAICE	Logicware Inc.	IBM, DEC VAX, Sun, Apollo, Tektronix	Rules

Induction Systems

Another major category of expert system shells are induction systems. These systems allow you to build an expert system by giving the program a series of examples. In this case, an example is a series of attributes or conditions that result in a specific outcome. During the knowledge engineering process the idea is to gather as many examples as possible from the domain of interest. The examples are entered into a matrix similar to that of a spreadsheet. Each column in the matrix represents a condition or attribute, with one representing the decisions, outcomes, or results that derive from the various combinations of attributes. The matrix is entered into the induction shell in much the same way that data is entered into a spreadsheet.

Once you list all possible examples, an algorithm inside the induction system generates rules from the matrix. In other words, rules are inferred from the data in the table. The resulting rules are either similar in structure to standard IF-THEN rules or are presented in decision-tree format from which rules are readily derived. A rule base is created using this process. From that point on, the standard inference engine uses the rule base to draw its conclusions during consultation.

Figure 6-3 shows examples entered into a matrix. A typical rule derived from example 4 in this table is shown here.

IF	the AC input is ok
AND	the secondary voltage is zero
AND	the filter output is zero
AND	the regulator output is zero
THEN	the problem is a bad fuse

**Figure 6-3.
Matrix of Examples
from which Rules Are
Derived**

	acin	secvolt	filout	regout	Result
1:	ok	ok	norm	zero	openreg
2:	ok	ok	low	low	badcap
3:	ok	ok	zero	zero	badrect
4:	ok	zero	zero	zero	badfuse
5.	ok	ok	norm	high	shortreg

power supply troubleshooting expert system

Induction shells are much easier to use than rule-based shells.

The main benefit of an induction shell is its ease of use. Creating the rules from the collected knowledge is sometimes difficult, but creating the matrix of attributes and outcomes is quite simple. The expert may be able to create the matrix, thus greatly minimizing the complex and time-consuming knowledge engineering process.

The induction algorithm in the shell examines the matrix and helps to eliminate redundant information. Once all of the examples have been analyzed, some of the attributes may be found to be unnecessary for drawing a conclusion. In *Figure 6-3*, the "acin" (alternating current input) attribute is of no value since it is the same in all examples. As a result, it can be eliminated from the rule given above. In addition, not all examples must result in an individual rule. By looking for patterns and combining them properly and by eliminating attributes, the induction algorithm can minimize the rule set.

During the induction process, a decision tree based on the examples is derived. A decision tree for the data in *Figure 6-3* is shown in *Figure 6-4*. You can see how the nodes in the tree are related to the rules. We'll discuss this example in some detail in Chapter 7.

Figure 6-4. Decision Tree Derived from Matrix in Figure 6-3

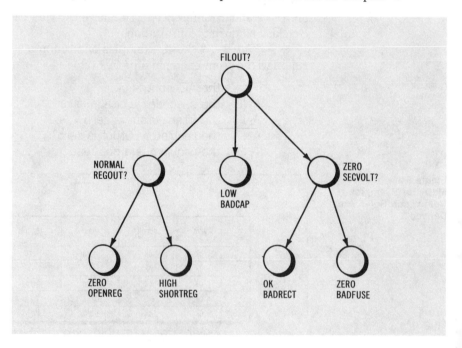

Because of the simplicity of the induction process, it can be used as a way of learning how to write your own rules from scratch.

When building an induction shell, be sure to use a sufficient number of examples in order to ensure accurate decisions. If only a few examples are used, the inferred rules may not be general enough to apply to all of the conditions encountered.

It is also desirable to use as many attributes as possible in describing each example. All of the attributes may not be necessary, but it is difficult to determine this when putting together the matrix. Should an attribute turn out to be unnecessary in drawing a conclusion, the induction algorithm will eliminate it for you.

This description of induction shells gives you a clue to one of the techniques used in creating expert systems with a rule-based shell. That method, of course, is to format your knowledge into examples and create a matrix. From the matrix, then, you can infer most of the rules yourself. We'll expand upon that technique in Chapter 7.

Shell Specifications and Features

Prior to purchasing a shell, you must consider a number of specifications and features. By looking at the details of a variety of shells, you can compare them and select the one that best fits your situation. In this section we list the most important specifications and features.

Operating Environment

This refers to the computer and its operating system which act as host for the shell. A description of the operating environment will indicate the computer manufacturer, type and model number of the computer, the operating system, and any relevant hardware limitations. These latter may include number and type of disk drives, the amount of RAM needed, and so on.

Type of Shell

A description of the shell will indicate whether it is of the rule-based or induction type. There are many more rule-based systems than induction systems. Many of the rule-based systems permit other forms of knowledge representation such as frames and semantic networks. And some induction systems let you write your own rules.

Shell Language

This is the programming language in which the shell is implemented. Most shells are written in structured high-level languages such as Pascal and C. Several have been written in BASIC and FORTRAN. A good number of shells have also been written in LISP and Prolog. Since most LISPs and Prologs are interpreters, they must be resident in the machine, requiring a considerable amount of additional memory space. Programs written in compilers do not require a resident program.

Control System

Choose a control strategy based on your problem.

The control system refers to the method of search used by the inference engine. Most shells use either forward- or backward-chaining but some of the more sophisticated shells allow you to choose one or the other or both concurrently in the problem-solving phase. While most expert systems can be implemented using either approach, one approach may be preferable for certain problems. During the expert system development stage, you want to determine the best inferencing method so that you can match that to the shell.

The control strategy will also include deciding how uncertainty will be handled. Most rule-based systems use certainty factors, while only a few use probability or fuzzy logic. Again, you should determine during the early stages of development which method of inexact reasoning might be best for your problem. Beware of shells with no capability for handling uncertainty. Most real-world domains need this capability.

Mathematical Capability

Some shells have computational capability that allows them to do mathematical operations. Your problems may require calculations on input data prior to a search of the rule base. Be sure to check the mathematical capability of the shell before buying.

Software Hooks

A very useful feature is to be able to link to other software.

A desirable feature on a shell is the ability to link to other applications software packages, such as spreadsheets or data base management systems. Some expert systems also have built-in "hooks" for use with a graphics program, allowing presentation of results in graphical form. Another hook might link you to a language that can call the expert system and vice versa.

Programming Languages

Often a shell will be accompanied by a programming language. This is helpful if the shell does not meet all of your requirements. Expert systems implemented in LISP and Prolog typically allow access to these languages. The result is that you may combine the features of the shell with specially created programs using the built-in language so that you can customize the shell to your application. Many of the available languages are unique to a particular manufacturer.

User Interface

The user interface describes the user-to-machine communications. For example, how does the shell conduct a consultation? Does it present questions to be answered, or does it present menus with multiple choices? How is material presented on the video display? Does the system use color or windows?

Special Considerations

Table 6-7 lists several additional considerations in shell selection. These include price, run-time versions, royalties, vendor assistance, and documentation.

Table 6-7.
Special Shell
Specifications

Specification	Description
Price	Shells for PCs are priced from $50–$10,000. Shells for minis run from $10,000–$100,000.
Run-Time Version	The inference engine, knowledge base, and user interface required to run the expert system. Knowledge input subsystem is not included, so no development or maintenance can be done. Cheaper than the full shell, these are the best choice for distributing many copies of an expert system.
Royalties	Some vendors require a royalty or use fee on distribution copies of expert systems using their shell. Can be a major expense if many copies of the expert system are to be distributed.
Vendor Assistance	Reliable vendors support the shell and help users with telephone "hot" lines, customer training, and other services.
Documentation	Good documentation can ease your learning and use of a shell and help you get the most from your investment.

TYPICAL SHELLS

To give you a feel for the commercial shells available, we'll examine two popular shells for the IBM PC. One is an induction type, the other is rule-based. These are representative of other PC shells.

1st Class

This is an induction system developed and sold by Programs in Motion, Inc., in Wayland, MA. A complete list of specifications is given in *Table 6-8*.

Table 6-8.
1st Class

Specification	Description
Operating Environment	IBM PC or compatible; 256K RAM, 512K preferred; one floppy or hard disk; PC/MS-DOS Version 2.0 or higher
Type of Shell	Induction with example weights
Shell Implementation Language	Pascal and assembler
Control System	Backward-chaining
Mathematical Capability	None
Software Hooks	Can interface with ASCII and 1-2-3 files and most word processors; can link to any language; full DOS access.
User Interface	Color, menus, and windows; limited use of function keys
Price	$495; demo package $20
Run-Time Version	None available or required
Royalties or Fees	None
Vendor Assistance	Phone help
Documentation	375-page manual with tutorial; demo and intro disks

This shell is very easy to use. Knowledge is entered as examples—up to 240—in a matrix. You can use up to 32 attributes and up to 32 outcomes. If you need more space, you can divide the knowledge base into logical segments with the size limits just given and link them. A certainty factor-like value called a weight (0–1.0 scale) can be added to each result to deal with ambiguous knowledge.

You can also enter rules directly with a decision tree format. This lets you control which questions are asked, what input data is solicited, and how it is used.

If you use examples as the knowledge base, 1st Class will infer the rules and decision tree for you. You saw an example of this in *Figures 6-3* and *6-4*. You have four choices from which to choose.

1. Optimize—eliminates attributes and related questions that don't affect the result. Then it puts the remaining factors into a sequence that asks the fewest questions. The resulting optimized rule saves you time and runs faster by asking fewer questions.

2. Left-Right—like the Optimize choice, this method also eliminates unnecessary attributes. It differs by asking questions from left to right in an order that you establish.

3. Customize—enables you build the rule tree yourself.

4. Match—similar to a standard data base search. Instead of generating a decision tree, the inference engine asks the user every question, in left-to-right order of the associated attributes. If the user's response is identical to any examples you entered, the corresponding results are shown. Otherwise, the result is "no-data."

To use 1st Class after the knowledge base is created, you initiate an advisory session. The program presents multiple-choice questions based upon the attributes in the matrix. The choices are the attribute values you entered. After you answer all the questions, the inference engine has enough data to draw a conclusion. If you entered explanatory text when you created the matrix, it will be given with the questions or result, whichever is appropriate.

EXSYS

EXSYS is one of the oldest PC rule-based shells on the market. Developed by EXSYS, Inc., in Albuquerque, NM, it has been regularly updated and enhanced over the years. There is also a version that runs on the DEC VAX minicomputers under the VMS operating system. EXSYS is easy to use and results in fast, compact expert systems. *Table 6-9* lists the basic specifications.

**Table 6-9.
EXSYS**

Specification	Description
Operating Environment	IBM PC or compatible; 256K RAM minimum; one floppy or hard disk drive; PC/MS-DOS Version 2.0 or higher
Type of Shell	Production rules with confidence factors
Shell Language	C
Control System	Backward- or forward-chaining
Mathematical Capabilities	Supports $+$, $-$, $*$, $/$ as well as $=$, $>$, $<$, $\geq$, $\leq$ and $<>$; also logs, trig, exponentials, and square roots.
Software Hooks	To other languages as well as applications programs
User Interface	Color, windows, and menus
Price	$395
Run-Time Version	Yes
Royalties or Fees	$600 for one-time unlimited license to distribute products
Vendor Assistance	Phone help
Documentation	100-page manual; two demo disks with tutorial

The knowledge base is created by entering rules directly. The standard IF-THEN format is used. An optional ELSE clause can also be added to the rules although it isn't normally needed. As with other rules, the THEN outcome is true, assuming the IF conditions are true. When the IF conditions aren't true, the ELSE clause is fired or true.

There are three optional methods of handling uncertainty in EXSYS. A 0 or 1 scale can be used for false/true, no/yes situations. A 0–10 scale is also available where 0 is absolutely false or no while 10 is definitely true or yes. The 1–9 values represent intermediate degrees of falsity or truth. The third, and most sophisticated, method is a -100 to $+100$ scale which provides greater precision in defining the confidence of the outcomes.

You enter rules with the built-in text editor. The screen is divided into windows for entering rule clauses. One window contains prompts and command choices. The editor makes it easy to add or change the rules, and it links to the run-time module so that you can easily test your rules as you write them.

Assuming an average rule of 7 clauses divided among the IF and THEN parts, you can write about 700 rules per 64K of RAM over 192K. In other words, you could run a 700-rule knowledge base in 256K RAM. With a full 640K on a PC, almost 5000 total rules could be used—an enormous figure, especially for a PC. Most mini and mainframe expert systems are rarely this large.

A consultation session with EXSYS is fast and easy. The system asks multiple-choice questions to gather the data input necessary for a decision. The inference engine then backward-chains to produce a solution.

What Have We Learned?

1. A "tool" is software that aids in the creation of an expert system or other AI program. The two main tool choices are programming languages and shells.

2. Any conventional programming language can be used to create an expert system, but structured languages such as Pascal are preferred. C is the language of choice among those using traditional languages.

3. Symbolic languages LISP and Prolog are superior tools for creating expert systems and other AI programs.

4. LISP is not only the second oldest high-level programming language but also the most powerful and flexible language for creating AI software.

5. Most symbolic knowledge can be put into a list format: objects arranged in a logical grouping or order. LISP is a language designed to manipulate lists. Search and pattern-matching can be readily implemented.

6. Lists are made up of individual elements called atoms which may be numerical data or symbols. The list is defined by enclosing the atoms within parentheses.

7. Lists are processed by procedures. Primitives are procedures, such as math operators, contained within LISP. Predicates are primitives and make true-false decisions.

8. A major benefit of LISP is that new procedures may be created to manipulate lists in any way desired.

9. LISP is available for most popular PCs, minicomputers, and mainframes.

10. The second most popular AI language is Prolog. Prolog is a declarative language that lets you state facts but not procedures for solving a problem.

11. In Prolog, you create a knowledge base of facts and rules. Prolog's built-in inference engine backward chains to draw conclusions.

12. Many special AI languages have been created but few are practical commercial products. One exception is Smalltalk, an object-based language whose use in AI work is growing.

13. The most useful tool for creating an expert system is a shell or expert system generator. It consists of all the standard parts of an expert system except that it has an empty knowledge base. Users create their own knowledge bases without programming.

14. The two main types of shells are the induction type and the rule-based type. The rule-based type is more common. Some also permit frame knowledge bases to be created.

15. Induction shells let you enter knowledge as examples in a matrix format. The shell then infers rules that are used by the inference engine to reach a conclusion.

16. Many shells are available for the IBM PC and its compatibles. Shells can also be obtained for minis and mainframes.

17. Some important specifications and features to consider in comparing and selecting shells are operating environment; type of shell; shell implementation language; control strategy, including uncertainty capability; math capability; software hooks; user interface; price; run-time version; royalties; user support; and documentation.

Quiz for Chapter 6

1. A "tool" is a(n):
   a. applications program.
   b. language.
   c. shell.
   d. b and c above.

2. The preferred conventional high-level language for creating AI software is:
   a. Forth.
   b. Pascal.
   c. C.
   d. FORTRAN.

3. Which of the following is *not* an AI programming language?
   a. LISP.
   b. Forth.
   c. Smalltalk.
   d. Prolog.

4. The most widely used AI programming language is:
   a. LISP.
   b. C.
   c. Prolog.
   d. Smalltalk.

5. LISP and Prolog are usually implemented as:
   a. shells.
   b. compilers.
   c. interpreters.
   d. utilities.

6. The advantage of an AI program written in C over a LISP program is:
   a. speed of execution.
   b. ease of development.
   c. modularity.
   d. C is more available than LISP.

7. The basic data or knowledge structure in LISP is:
   a. rules.
   b. lists.
   c. frames.
   d. semantic nets.

8. Prolog is used to implement a(n):
   a. knowledge base.
   b. inference engine.
   c. procedural language.
   d. algorithm.

9. The basic data or knowledge structure in Prolog is:
   a. primitives and predicates.
   b. facts and rules.
   c. lists and trees.
   d. functions and procedures.

10. When LISP evaluates the expression ((CAR '(A B C D)), it will return:
   a. (B C D).
   b. C.
   c. A.
   d. (A B C).

11. When LISP evaluates the predicate (EQUAL (STOP)(SPOT)), it will return:
   a. T.
   b. NIL.
   c. STOP.
   d. SPOT.

12. The correct format for the Prolog fact "Hilda loves Hans" is:
   a. loves (Hilda,Hans).
   b. Hilda (loves,Hans).
   c. Hans (loved__by Hilda).
   d. loves (hilda,hans).

13. In a Prolog rule, the symbol
:- means:
- **a.** IF.
- **b.** THEN.
- **c.** ELSE.
- **d.** AND.

14. A shell is an expert system
without a(n):
- **a.** knowledge base.
- **b.** inference engine.
- **c.** user interface.
- **d.** explanation capability.

15. The basic knowledge
structure of an induction shell
is a(n):
- **a.** tree.
- **b.** matrix.
- **c.** rule set.
- **d.** semantic net.

16. The better rule-based shells
have a(n):
- **a.** induction capability.
- **b.** forward-chaining inference
  engine.
- **c.** way to express
  uncertainty.
- **d.** text editor.

17. Most shells deal with
ambiguity by using:
- **a.** probability.
- **b.** fuzzy logic.
- **c.** priority weights.
- **d.** certainty factors.

18. The most common shell
control strategy is:
- **a.** rule induction.
- **b.** backward-chaining.
- **c.** semantic net search
- **d.** forward-chaining.

19. Which of the following
features allows shells to link
to other software?
- **a.** Windows.
- **b.** Math capability.
- **c.** Software hooks.
- **d.** Certainty factors.

20. Users writing an expert
system in a shell, then
distributing multiple copies
may have to:
- **a.** pay royalties or fees.
- **b.** revise the program as
  new versions become
  available.
- **c.** use a language to enhance
  it.
- **d.** ask for vendor permission.

How to Develop an Expert System

ABOUT THIS CHAPTER

Developing an expert system is similar to developing any computer software. The problem has to be defined, appropriate solutions identified, program code written, testing and debugging performed. The primary difference between creating an expert system and more conventional software is the step called knowledge engineering. The heart of the expert system is the knowledge of the domain, which is formatted into a knowledge base appropriate for the project. Knowledge engineering is the most difficult part of the development process.

In this chapter we'll examine the ten basic steps involved in creating an expert system. With this information, you should have a good feel for what is involved and whether you are interested in tackling such a project.

TEN STEPS TO AN EXPERT SYSTEM

The steps you must take to develop an expert system are enumerated here. In the following sections, we'll study each of the steps in the process and then we'll examine two sample expert systems.

1. Define the problem
2. Evaluate alternative solutions
3. Verify an expert system solution
4. Estimate the payoff
5. Choose an expert system tool
6. Perform the knowledge engineering
7. Build the knowledge base
8. Develop the software
9. Test and validate the system
10. Maintain the system

Step 1: Define the Problem

This is the first step in any software development project. This problem-identification stage is critical before you invest a lot of time and money in development work. A clear problem definition simplifies the remaining steps significantly and helps you generate a productive program.

Don't develop any software until you know what the true need is.

Defining the problem is a matter of answering some basic questions. Just what is the problem? The real need? Typical problems could be low productivity, lack of sufficient expert knowledge to go around, information overload, time problems, or people problems. Whatever the problem or need, write a clear statement of it and provide as much supporting information as possible. This statement will serve as the guideline and specification for your development program.

Expert systems are a solution looking for a problem.

Expert system technology is relatively new and many people are still discovering it. It is a fascinating subject and one that is catching the attention of almost everyone who uses computers. For that reason, people are inclined to seek problems that an expert system can solve just so that they can get involved with the technology. While there is nothing wrong with this approach, keep in mind that the real issue is to solve the problem in the best way; an expert system may or may not be the correct solution.

Most expert systems are being used to improve an aspect of poor job performance. For example, an employee may not be achieving a desired quantity or quality of work within time or cost constraints. Problems like this can often be traced to a lack of knowledge. The employee must either possess the knowledge or have access to it, whether in the form of an expert person or an expert system.

Do a job or task analysis to find out what the problem is.

The best way to get a handle on the problem or need is to do a kind of formal study called a "needs assessment" or "job/task analysis." With this, the suspected performance problem is revealed and analyzed. The analysis may entail observations of the employee doing the job and interviews with the employee, the supervisor, or perhaps even customers, which may give indications of the nature of the problem. Gather all information related to the job, such as job descriptions and performance standards, that the personnel department can provide.

As we have seen, knowledge is at the heart of those problems that best fit expert system solutions. What does the employee know? What is his or her educational background, training, and experience? Are experts accessible?

Of course, not all problems are going to be related to poor employee performance. But, despite the kind of problem, collecting relevant background information is important because it gives you the data you need to make a decision about a development program. If knowledge is at the root of the problem, you most likely have a candidate for an expert system.

Step 2: Evaluate Alternative Solutions

Depending upon the problem, you usually have several solution options in addition to expert systems.

Before jumping into a major expert system development program, you should consider alternative solutions to the problem. Lack of knowledge is a problem that could be solved in other ways. Let's consider some examples.

Make Experts Available

If the problem is knowledge related, then someone must have the desired knowledge. One approach may simply be to make the expert more accessible to those needing the expertise. This might be as simple as making the expert's telephone number available to the person needing it. Another solution might be to identify additional experts who can help. Hiring or creating new experts is another option.

Education and Training

One approach to a knowledge crisis is to create new experts.

An individual acquires knowledge through study and experience. One solution is to provide additional education and training in the desired subject matter for those who need it. Appropriate courses or seminars may be available. If not, the experts could create and teach them. Employees could work with experts to acquire the knowledge and experience through on-the-job training. This solution creates new experts through education.

Even if training and education are the best solution, of course, there will be some development cost. But courses, seminars, and related materials are much less expensive to develop than an expert system. Another cost savings may be that the employee won't need a computer.

Training and education are excellent long-term solutions because, having acquired them, the employee usually retains their benefits. Remember, though, that should the employee leave the job, the knowledge would be lost. Creating an expert system containing the knowledge is a superior permanent solution but it is far more time-consuming and expensive than training. You have to weigh these trade-offs to discover the best approach.

Packaging Knowledge

An alternative to additional education and training is to package the knowledge and related information into printed documentation. The expert may be able to create or help create a manual or job aid containing all the facts, figures, procedures, and other knowledge needed to do the job. In this form, an employee can readily access it. Many times this simple solution is all that is required.

An alternative to a manual is a job aid, a concise printed form or document that reduces the necessary knowledge and information to short lists, step-by-step procedures, tables, flow charts, graphs, and other structured information. A job aid must be short and simple so that the information and knowledge can be rapidly accessed.

Again, it takes time to generate manuals and job aids. However, they are far less expensive than expert systems and a great deal faster and easier to create.

Conventional Software

A conventional software solution should be considered before an expert system.

A computer solution may still be best for your problem, but an expert system might not be completely appropriate. Once you've defined your problem, you should examine the possibility of using existing standard software packages. For example, a spreadsheet or data base management system may work. The decision software programs we discussed in Chapter 4 may also be a better fit to your particular problem. Alternately, you may wish to consider developing a special algorithmic program that solves the problem. If you have the ability to develop traditional software, you should evaluate this option. It may be a faster and simpler solution than an expert system. This is particularly true if expert systems are new to you and your organization, because there is a large overhead associated with creating the first expert system as it is a learning process. However, if an expert system is a good fit for the solution and there is general agreement to make the investment, then by all means do it.

If you are a lawyer, you tend to see the solution to every problem as legal action. If you are an instructional designer, you probably see training as the solution to every problem. Expert system developers should strive to avoid this syndrome. Keep in mind that you have choices. Try to be open-minded and objective in analyzing alternatives. It is the solution that is important, not the means of reaching it.

Step 3: Verify an Expert System Solution

Assume that you have concluded that this is indeed a problem that could be solved with an expert system. One more step is required before going ahead with development; you must be sure that the problem is a good fit to an expert system.

To determine the suitability of your problem, try to match it up to one of the categories we discussed in Chapter 2. These key application areas are suitable for expert systems. They are summarized here.

1. Analysis and interpretation
2. Prediction
3. Diagnosis and debugging
4. Monitoring and control
5. Design
6. Planning
7. Instruction

If your problem falls into one of these categories, then you can begin thinking in terms of an expert system.

But wait—a few more conditions must be satisfied. These conditions are listed here.

1. Knowledge required to solve problem
2. Experts available
3. Narrow domain
4. Symbolic knowledge
5. High return on investment
6. No common sense needed
7. Moderate problem difficulty
8. Requires cognitive solution
9. Reasonable number of outcomes

Expert Knowledge Required

A problem suitable for an expert system solution must meet special conditions.

We have mentioned this before, but it bears repeating. If your problem cannot be solved with expert knowledge, then obviously an expert system is a poor solution choice. If having another human expert would solve your problem, then an expert system is probably a good choice. Your dilemma may be that you simply do not have enough experts to go around.

Keep in mind, too, that your objective may be to preserve the knowledge of a retiring, resigning, or transferring expert. An expert system may be the only way to capture this valuable knowledge so that it can be learned and used by others.

Think of all those conditions where knowledge is required to deal with a human overload condition. Many problems require the rapid and accurate analysis of a large amount of information. Expert systems are great for this type of problem.

And don't forget those applications where expert systems may be built into special computers such as those in weapons or factory controllers. In any case, the key need must be knowledge.

Availability of Experts

You can't develop an expert system unless the human expertise is available to contribute to it. In most cases, you need only one expert, but in some cases the desired knowledge resides with more than one individual. You must have access to these people to create the expert system.

A willing expert is the main requirement for a successful expert system.

Another important factor is that the experts should be willing to contribute to the development effort. Some experts may be reluctant because they haven't the time or the desire to share their knowledge. A willing participant is essential to a successful expert system development program.

Narrow Domain

Expert systems must be narrow and focused, not broad and general.

Another major requirement is that the domain knowledge be narrow and precise. In other words, to create a successful expert system you must focus on a specific subject. Broad general subjects don't make good expert systems; the expert systems would be too large and difficult to create. If your problem zeros in on a very definite topic, it is most likely appropriate.

The Nature of the Knowledge

The kind of knowledge suitable for an expert system is that which can be represented in symbolic form. You must be able to convert the knowledge into IF-THEN rules, frames, or another knowledge representation scheme. Remember that the most useful knowledge is the heuristic type gained from years of experience in practical problem-solving. The trick is to format that heuristic knowledge in a way that it can be represented in a computer. Before going ahead with a development project, you should make a first attempt at identifying a small segment of the knowledge and try to adapt it to one of the well-known methods of symbolic representation.

High Return on Investment

Developing any expert system is going to take time and cost money. This investment must be worth the result. If you cannot determine that you will receive a worthwhile return on your investment, you should reconsider using an expert system. You'll appreciate that the greater the return on investment, the easier it is to get the funding and support to develop your expert system.

No Need for Common Sense

Expert systems cannot deal with common sense.

Because common sense is made up of a lot of individual pieces of unrelated knowledge, expert systems can't solve problems requiring common sense. Common sense covers such a broad range of subjects that you could never list them all. Common sense knowledge means that you know that the sky is blue and that you will get wet if you go out into the rain. Common sense tells you not to step in front of a speeding truck. There is no way that all such knowledge can be programmed into an expert system. Therefore, if your problem requires common sense knowledge for solution, you should seriously consider abandoning the project. Expert systems are good only at solving problems related to a very specific domain.

Solution Difficulty

Problems that are not too easy or too hard are best for expert systems.

If the knowledge required to solve a problem is limited and the solutions tend to be extremely simple, then you probably don't need an expert system. One of the alternatives we discussed earlier may be a better fit. An expert system may also be a bad solution if the problem is extremely large and complex. If the required knowledge is enormous and its application difficult, an expert system may not be up to the job. Expert systems appear to solve problems of moderate difficulty between those two extremes.

One way to judge this is to try to estimate the amount of time it will take an expert to solve the problem. If the expert solves the problem in a few minutes, it is probably too simple. If the problem takes many hours to solve, it may be too difficult. A solution that requires between ten minutes and three hours is probably a good expert system working range.

Cognitive Solutions

Expert systems perform mental, not physical, work.

As we've seen, expert systems attempt to duplicate the mental processes of an expert individual. Your problem must be one that can be solved by thinking and reasoning. If you've met the knowledge requirements described earlier, this is probably the case. Expert systems don't have the senses, such as sight, hearing, and touch, to solve physical problems. Neither do they have manipulative skills. If your problem requires such inputs and outputs, you should rethink your solution.

Expert system and artificial intelligence technology has reached the point where it may be possible to give expert systems some of these physical qualities. For example, computer vision systems provide a form of sight and speech recognition systems simulate hearing. Depending upon your application, it may be possible to integrate such systems with your expert system software to solve your problem. You may not need even these relatively sophisticated senses in cases when standard sensors or transducers can provide electrical input signals to the computer. In some applications all you may need is to sense temperature, pressure, liquid level, physical position, speed, presence of light or infrared, or another characteristic. Transducers can provide a simple form of simulated human sensing.

In the same way, expert system outputs may also be translated into electrical signals that can perform limited control and manipulation, such as controlling a manipulator arm or another form of robot. In simpler cases, control signals could operate relays, solenoids, lights, motors, or other electronic or electromechanical devices.

Unless your need is overwhelming and experience is great, however, it is probably best to stick with an expert system requiring only mental processes to solve the problem.

Reasonable Number of Outcomes

The expert system that you create is going to generate a solution or a recommendation. When building the expert system, you'll need to know what each of the possible outcomes is. They will be programmed into the expert system and the search process ultimately will lead to one of them. The best expert systems are those that contain a moderate number of solutions. If the total number of solutions is few, you probably don't need an expert system. A decision between two or three choices, for instance, might be more easily made by a human.

If there are hundreds or even thousands of possible outcomes, an expert system is going to find it difficult to accommodate them. A successful expert system probably has an upper limit of about a hundred solutions.

Step 4: Estimating the Payoff

Don't develop an expert system unless the payoff is high.

Expert systems are expensive to develop. Like most other software projects, you'll make a major investment of time and money creating a workable program. Knowing some of the costs involved helps you estimate the payoff.

Getting a Handle on Development Costs

First, factor in the cost of any expert system development tools, such as languages and shells. Next, consider what new hardware you might need. Will you need additional computers, terminals, disk drives, or other hardware for development and later application?

The people costs will be your major investment.

Include the cost of the expert in your development estimates if that expert is not already on your payroll. You'll generally need a knowledge engineer and a programmer although for a simple expert system, you may not need the knowledge engineer, and if a shell is to be used, you may not need the programmer. Don't forget to include the time needed for employees to test, debug, and maintain the program. Finally, add in costs for outside consultants that may be needed.

The secret to making a realistic estimate lies in determining the amount of time each of the participants will spend. This is particularly true for software developers, who invariably are optimistic in the amount of time they will need to complete a project. Unless an individual has considerable software development experience and a good track record, it is almost inevitable that he or she will assume that it can be done a lot faster than it will actually take. It is not unrealistic to double or triple the time estimates you have been given or that you have developed. This is especially true for a first expert system. If you'll be learning the process as you go, expect to spend more time than estimated, particularly in the knowledge engineering phase.

It is practically impossible to make the perfect estimate, but it is essential that an estimate of development costs be made. Even an educated guess is better than none at all.

A small system with less than a hundred rules may take only several months and require two or three people at most. Still, developing such a project could cost from $10,000 to $50,000. If you use an inexpensive shell on a personal computer and create a small expert system, you may be able to do it for several thousand dollars, assuming that your expert will also do the knowledge engineering and program the knowledge into the shell.

If you are planning a large expert system for a minicomputer or a mainframe, your cost will be above $100,000. Even shells for larger computers are expensive; the smaller shells sell for about $10,000, but most are priced in the $20,000–60,000 range. The addition of knowledge engineering puts the cost above $100,000. To justify such costs, the proposed system has to be extremely beneficial.

Evaluating the Benefits

Benefits may be tangible or intangible.

While estimating development costs is difficult at best, estimating the payoff will probably be even harder. As we indicated earlier, the benefits must be significant to justify the development of an expert system. If the payoff doesn't exceed your development costs, there is little reason to develop the expert system. In order to get approval to create an expert system, the return on your investment must be sufficiently high.

The key is in putting your finger on the benefits. If the expert system can solve a problem whose losses are currently known, you have a starting point. Otherwise, you have to try to calculate a dollar value for the benefits.

An expert system will generate income for you or prevent the loss of income. For example, having an expert system may allow you to do more work in less time, thus bringing in more revenue. You gain through improved productivity.

Most expert systems seem to eliminate losses rather than generate new income. The expert system may minimize wasted time or wasted materials. Poor service due to lack of knowledge may be causing the loss of sales and poor quality may be ruining your image and the trust your customers have for your work. If the expert system helps improve your reputation and reliability, it may bring new business.

Estimating the value of the benefits derived from an expert system may be almost impossible for some applications. The expert system is preserving valuable knowledge, but it is difficult to estimate the value of that knowledge. How would you determine the strategic superiority of an expert system-based weapon in terms of dollars and cents? Obviously, the strategic advantage is a benefit but putting a dollar figure on it is very difficult. The same is true of expert systems that save human lives or perform other functions whose value is nearly incalculable.

Amortizing development costs over a longer period makes the payoff relatively higher.

If your income or savings exceed development costs, an expert system is viable. Also, the expert system development cost is basically a one-time charge while the benefits may accrue for years, so you may wish to amortize the cost of development over several years to improve the return on your investment.

Step 5: Choose an Expert System Tool

Your application and internal capabilities will help you decide between a language and a shell.

Choosing which software tool to use is a major decision in the development process. Your choice will depend on several important factors. For example, is programming capability available in-house and, if so, which languages are used? What type of computer system will be used to develop the software and what is the user's host computer? The selection of tool will also be affected by the time and funds available to create the software. Will you use a shell, an AI language, or a conventional programming language? Finally, the selection will be greatly influenced by the nature of the problem itself.

Shells vs. Languages

Analyze your in-house software development capability. If you have a programming staff, identify workable languages and try to match those languages with tools that can run on your computers. Programmers should be able to write code quickly if they are familiar with the language. Remember, though, that programming an expert system from scratch is an enormous undertaking.

Another option is to consider adding AI programming language capability. If the project has sufficient funding and if future systems are to be designed and built, it may be worthwhile to have the programmers learn LISP or Prolog. Using these languages gives you a general AI capability. But again, keep in mind that it takes time to learn the languages well enough to create an expert system with them.

The fastest and easiest approach is to use a shell. But is there a shell made for your computer? Does the shell format fit the domain of interest? Is the shell large enough and capable enough to handle the project you have in mind?

If this is your first expert system development project, you should strive for a shell. Start by identifying shells available for your kind of computer, which we reviewed in Chapter 6. Most shells run on only a few target machines. Dozens of packages are available for the IBM Personal Computer and its various compatibles, fewer programs are available for the Apple Macintosh series, and fewer still are available for other personal computers. For minicomputers and mainframes, the choices are generally limited to IBM mainframes and DEC VAX minis.

If a shell is available for your computers and within budget, you need to determine if its capabilities fit your problem. You may have to do some initial knowledge engineering to see if the domain can be expressed properly in rule format. Match the specifications of the tool to other aspects of the problem, and if there is a fit, by all means make the investment.

If no shell exists for your machine or your knowledge domain doesn't fit rule format, your second choice should be the AI languages of Prolog or LISP. LISP and Prolog interpreters are available for almost any machine. Prolog is the better choice because, in general, it is easier to create an expert system in Prolog than it is in LISP. Prolog has a built-in inference engine and all you need to do is properly format the knowledge in terms of facts and rules. LISP also has an inference engine, but with LISP you have to implement search, pattern-matching, and other system features from scratch. Unless there is some major overriding consideration that forces the use of a conventional language, stay with LISP or Prolog if a shell is not available.

In summary, use these guidelines to choose a tool:

1. Shell—your best bet
2. Prolog—tougher than a shell, but easier than LISP
3. LISP—easier than a conventional language
4. Conventional Language—a last resort; choose only if application requires it

Shell Guidelines

When selecting a shell, you'll need to make a choice between induction and rule-based shells. If an induction shell fits your problem, choose it over the rule-based shell because development will be quicker and easier.

Another factor to consider is the shell size, usually determined by the number of production rules that can be used. Most shells have upper limits on the number of examples that can be entered or the number of rules they can handle. These limits are usually determined by the tool design and by the RAM and disk storage limitations of the host computer. Doing your knowledge engineering prior to selecting the tool gives you this information, enabling you to match your application to the tool.

Expert systems with over 500 rules are generally not possible or practical on a personal computer.

Table 7-1 gives a general guideline of system sizes. Typically, if a system requires more than 500 rules, the application is not suitable for personal computers. That guideline is blurring, however, as personal computers move from 16- to 32-bit designs and as their processing speeds and storage capacities increase. The newer personal computers based on the 80386 and 68020 32-bit microprocessors are certainly capable of dealing with large programs. This is a direct function of the shell software, which must take advantage of the processor's capabilities. For example, the EXSYS shell is capable of handling up to 5000 rules in a standard IBM PC or compatible.

Table 7-1.
Expert System Sizes

System Size	Number of Rules
Small	10–200
Medium	200–500
Large	Over 500

Another guideline you may find helpful in selecting a rule-based shell is that each rule typically occupies from 100 to 1000 bytes of memory. The exact amount, of course, depends upon the complexity of the rule, its format, and the shell implementation language. For an average rule, you might estimate 500 bytes and use that as a guideline for determining memory requirements.

Another factor to consider is the rule size-speed trade-off. The larger the rule base, the slower the system will run. If many rules have to be searched to reach a conclusion, the response time may be sluggish, particularly on a PC. Small rule bases run quickly and produce excellent results. The actual running time will depend considerably on the control strategies used in the inference engine. A fixed control strategy such as only backward-chaining may fit a wide range of problems, but it may not be best for your situation. Expert system run times have been known to vary by factors of up to 100-to-1 by changing from forward- to backward-chaining or vice versa. A system that provides both control strategies is most desirable so that you can match it to your problem.

Buy the biggest and best shell you can afford.

A general rule for purchasing a shell is to buy one that is larger and more flexible than you require. Your estimates of shell requirements may be inaccurate, particularly on a first development project, and you may ultimately discover that the inexpensive shell you choose may not be up to the job. It is best to invest in one with large rule capabilities, control strategy options, and other features of flexibility.

Choose a reliable vendor that supplies good documentation, development support, and training. Don't forget to examine the requirements for royalties or fees. If royalties or fees must be paid, you can factor these into the development and/or distribution costs.

You may wish to defer this step of the development process until the next step, the knowledge engineering, is complete. Your knowledge base must fit the shell format. By doing the knowledge engineering first, you will get a solid indication as to what form the knowledge base must take. Then you can determine whether it fits the shell. If your knowledge domain doesn't lend itself to rule representation, a shell may be a poor choice. Sometimes you can make some simple initial attempts to format the knowledge as described earlier and make a calculated decision. You may find that you have to use a language, such as LISP and Prolog, to develop the system you want. In most cases, it won't hurt to delay the tool selection step until the knowledge engineering is done.

Step 6: Perform the Knowledge Engineering

The first five steps of the expert system development process are preliminary steps involving planning and preparation. The real work of developing the expert system occurs in this step—knowledge engineering.

Knowledge engineering is the process of gathering the desired knowledge from the experts and formatting it into a knowledge base. The typical knowledge engineer has a computer science and AI background with specific experience in developing expert systems. Not usually an expert in a particular domain, the knowledge engineer generally knows problem-solving processes. In addition, the knowledge engineer knows knowledge representation techniques and in some cases may actually be a programmer. The chief skill of the knowledge engineer is the ability to extract the knowledge from the expert, a difficult process we'll examine in detail in a later section.

Knowledge comes from two basic sources, the literature and the expert. Let's explore both sources and then discuss how the knowledge engineer compiles the knowledge base.

Research of the Literature

Printed materials form a base of knowledge you will use in developing your system.

We use "literature" to mean any source of documentation about the knowledge domain. In beginning to build an expert system, you first seek out all sources of knowledge covering your domain. These may be books, magazine articles, equipment manuals, rules and regulations, or even memos and job aids. Any printed information about the domain will probably be useful in putting together the knowledge base.

Assume you're going to develop an expert system for troubleshooting a radar unit. You might begin by acquiring all of the documentation for the radar unit itself: operational manuals, service manuals, technical manuals, and even the original engineering documentation and manufacturing documentation if it is available. This literature serves as your master source of knowledge. Yet, as you will discover, it is the knowledge from the human expert that will be instrumental in creating the knowledge base.

Ask the experts you plan to use what literature they use. Ask them to supply relevant documentation or point out sources they originally used in gaining their expertise. Don't overlook training materials as an additional source of information.

Once all this literature is available, review it to familiarize yourself with the content. It isn't necessary to read it all, but you should be aware of what's there so you can draw upon it as required.

Debriefing an Expert

Having access to an expert is one of the basic requirements in making a decision to go ahead. If you can't find that expert, or get ready access to the expert, you're in trouble. Most experts have full-time jobs and are kept busy. Typically, they cannot spare the time to help you create an expert system. On the other hand, if this software solves a major problem in the organization, then the management should support use of the expert at least part-time to aid in the software's creation. Consider yourself lucky if the expert can be assigned to the project full-time.

You can't have an expert system without a willing expert.

Another issue is the willing participation of the expert. Many experts are reluctant to share what they know. They may be protecting themselves or may be insecure. By giving up their knowledge, some experts feel devalued. Some experts may be downright hostile about the whole concept. If one expert is not cooperative, find another or try using two or more people who together know what the expert knows.

Remember, the experts are the source of the expert system. It is their knowledge that will be cloned, packaged, and disseminated. The quality of the expert system depends upon the quality of the expert's knowledge and how well the system is implemented. You won't be able to rely solely on printed literature because the best knowledge is obtained from personal experience.

No two experts solve a problem in the same way.

It is generally best to work with a single expert. The reason for this is that even though several experts may claim to know the same domain, their actual knowledge and problem-solving approaches may be considerably different. This is particularly true of how experts reason. Because no two experts reason in the same way, it is best to stick with one expert rather than try to resolve the conflicting approaches of multiple experts. If you cannot get along with just one expert, however, you'll have to debrief each expert and then attempt to consolidate the resulting knowledge into a composite form. One way to do this is to keep the experts separated from one another and extract the knowledge from them independently. Then use one of the experts as a judge and advisor. This expert will resolve conflicts, work out differences, and help you codify the knowledge into a usable form.

The knowledge engineer usually debriefs the experts over a period of time, slowly (but surely, we hope) drawing out the information. The knowledge engineer asks a set of questions related to the domain and then seeks explanations or how each expert goes about solving typical problems. The debriefing goal is to identify which chunks of knowledge the experts draw upon and what their individual logical reasoning processes are. Most experts don't really think about how they go about solving a problem, so it must be drawn from them by skillful interviewing.

This is a difficult part of knowledge engineering and it makes experts think about things they do not ordinarily need to think about. The danger is having the experts tell you things that aren't true. This doesn't mean an expert will supply incorrect knowledge, but that the expert, not knowing how he or she thinks, will tell you things you want to hear rather than things as they really are. Or, the expert may not know an answer and tell you something just to be cooperative. Trying to separate fact from fiction is the knowledge engineer's most difficult job. One solution to this problem is building up a good rapport with the expert. This can be accomplished if the knowledge engineering process is done gradually over a period of time.

During your debriefing sessions, you'll be taking notes of answers to your questions. If it doesn't make the expert uncomfortable, recording your interview is preferable. If your expert is on loan, every minute counts and you don't want to have to repeat interviews. By getting the session on tape, you can have it transcribed for later reference.

At some point in the debriefing process, you will want to begin converting the knowledge into rules or some other knowledge structure. For example, write several rules and test them out on the expert. Ask the expert to tell you whether they are valid.

Another approach to knowledge engineering is to observe the expert doing his or her job. If you can, tag along with the expert on an actual problem-solving mission. Watch exactly how he or she goes about identifying or verifying the problem and then working it through to a solution. This is a useful step and will give you some valuable clues about the knowledge required and how it is applied to the problem. Observation is a revealing process; often what you see won't conform to what the expert may have told you. If the differences are substantial, your interviews should seek to resolve them.

How do you learn to become a knowledge engineer? There really aren't any schools that teach this, although the process may be explained in graduate-level computer science courses on expert system development. Few knowledge engineers have taken such courses. Most learned by experience. Building an expert system will teach you most of what you need to know. The more systems you build, the better you will become at it.

Knowledge engineers are a scarce commodity. There are probably no more than several hundred of them in the United States. They are in demand and are paid very high salaries. Yet, for large expert system development projects, they are essential. For small systems, you can get along without them.

Step 7: Build the Knowledge Base

This step of the expert system development process is treated separately even though it is actually a part of the knowledge engineering stage. Once the knowledge has been acquired from the expert, it has to be formatted into a knowledge base. Here we want to describe the process of organizing that knowledge in such a way that it can be understood and then translated into rules or another form of knowledge representation.

Defining the Solutions

Defining and listing all outcomes is the first step in building the rule base.

The first step in organizing your domain knowledge is to list all of the possible solutions, outcomes, answers, or recommendations. You must identify the exact outputs that will be presented on the computer screen to the user. Expert systems don't suddenly create advice out of a flash of genius; they have to know every possible answer ahead of time.

Your interview sessions with your expert should have covered a sufficient range of different problem-solving examples so that all the possible outcomes are defined. In fact, this is one of the main objectives in the knowledge engineering process.

You should annotate each of these possible outcomes. The reason for this is that most expert systems are capable of explaining their output. Expert system shells usually provide a means of entering comments that will supplement or explain each output conclusion.

If you're using a rule-based system, each conclusion will be the THEN portion of a rule. At this point, you can begin creating the rules for each outcome. Some simple expert systems have a set of rules that define each outcome and that's it. The decisions are not reached through a complex search or a decision tree. Instead, the expert system simply asks questions to gather the necessary data for the IF statements that will fire one of the rules leading to a conclusion.

Define the Input Facts

The next step is to identify and list all of the data that will be required by the user. These are the facts and figures that the user will enter into the system. The expert system will actually ask questions to obtain these inputs. These facts and figures provide the IF statements for many of the rules in the system. The data provided by the user will be compared to IF statements in the rules to begin or continue the search process. With this information, you should be able to construct some of the rules that will ultimately lead to the conclusions.

Develop an Outline

Even though you may know the outcomes and needed input data, you may have difficulty writing the rules. Large complex knowledge domains usually require some additional organization in order to get a handle on them. One technique that may be useful is to develop an outline. Most domains lend themselves to some sort of taxonomy that will allow you to subdivide and classify the knowledge. An outline is nothing more than a hierarchy of these subdivisions.

A way to better picture the knowledge is to convert your outline into a block diagram. This will look somewhat like a company organizational chart. If you can organize your knowledge this way, you can feel comfortable that you are on the right track to building your knowledge base.

Draw a Decision Tree

The elements of knowledge may be such that they organize themselves quickly into a tree format. So, instead of making an outline, you may be able to go directly to the construction of a decision or search tree. In many cases, the knowledge will organize itself into rules with each node in the tree representing a rule.

Some knowledge bases are so large that you may not be able to create a decision tree for the entire domain. Don't worry about doing this. Create decision trees for subsets of the domain. You'll find a decision tree is a superior visual aid in helping you understand and organize the knowledge. Once you are comfortable with the fact that this format fits the knowledge base, you can dispense with the actual visualization and get on with the rule writing.

Map a Matrix

A matrix of examples is one of the best ways to organize some kinds of knowledge.

As we saw earlier, much knowledge organizes itself nicely into a matrix showing the various attributes that produce a particular conclusion. Induction shells use this knowledge formatting technique. If you have selected such a shell, you can proceed immediately to organizing your knowledge as examples. Regardless of the knowledge, organizing it using a matrix is one of the best ways to block it out and analyze it. Each column to the left of the right-most column represents an attribute. The right-most column designates the outcomes resulting from the occurrences of various combinations of attributes. Each row in the matrix is an example of the attributes leading to a specific outcome.

Once you have constructed the matrix, you can often write the rules directly from it. The attributes become the conditions in the IF portion of the rule. The outcome becomes the THEN portion. Of course, if you have an induction shell, these rules will be inferred directly from the matrix, saving you the trouble.

After you have used one or more of these techniques to organize and understand the knowledge, you write the IF-THEN rules. If you have already chosen a shell, you'll use the rule format specified.

The rule-writing task can be greatly simplified by subdividing the knowledge base into logical divisions. If you've developed an outline or decision tree, you can identify the subdivisions and begin working in the smaller areas, building gradually to large subdivisions. By taking this step-by-step process, you slowly but surely create the knowledge base. After you've committed the knowledge base to paper, you can begin creating the software.

Step 8: Develop the Software

Build a prototype to check the validity of your system.

Once your rules are written, you can enter them immediately into a shell. Your first objective should be to build a small prototype. Select one small subset of the knowledge base and enter its rules into the shell. You should be able to do this quickly. The result will be a prototype you can test in order to check your ideas and verify their implementation quickly. If your prototype works, you can proceed with confidence to enter the remainder of the rules.

Incidentally, a prototype is a good way to prove your concept before investing in a major program. If you use a shell, you can rapidly assemble a small prototype that will tell you if you're on the right track. A demonstration of the prototype can also be a valuable aid in acquiring approval and funding for your project.

The nice thing about rule-based systems is that they are modular. You can construct small subdivisions of larger systems and test them a step at a time, adding to the system in a piecemeal fashion and building to the final system gradually. By testing and approving each subsection separately, the final system should work the first time.

Another benefit of rule-based systems is that you can quickly make needed changes. You'll invariably make mistakes in creating the rule base and you'll find you need to modify rules, add new rules, remove rules, or make other changes. A rule-based system enables you to make these modifications easily.

Step 9: Test and Validate the System

Once you have built a prototype, you should try it out on your expert. Let the expert tell you if the results are satisfactory. You should also test it out on those who will actually use the system. The purpose of testing with experts and users is to validate the results. Does the expert system do what is intended? Does the system actually solve the problems that led to its development?

The testing and validation process is an important step in the development process. If you don't spend some time on this phase, the resulting product may be either worthless or provide insufficient help. The testing phase will usually turn up bugs or problems of some kind. With this kind of feedback, you can make the necessary corrections. This process may have to be repeated several times until all of the bugs are out and the system works as intended.

Large expert systems usually go through a series of development stages. The first stage is the demonstration prototype that shows that the system is viable. The system is put through several additional levels of development until it is considered a finished product. *Table 7-2* outlines these stages in the development process. Not all systems go through all of the stages.

**Table 7-2.
Stages of Expert
System Development**

Stage	Operation
Demonstration prototype	Shows viability using a subset
Research prototype	An operational first version of the entire system, but untested
Field prototype	A tested and reliable version
Production model	Demonstrates good performance in the user environment
Commercial system	Final version for sale or use

Step 10: Maintain the System

The development process doesn't end when your expert system goes into everyday use. While the system may be useful for an extended period of time, it may also become dated. Knowledge may change or become obsolete. The knowledge in your system may remain correct, but new knowledge may be discovered. Many domains are dynamic in that changes in the knowledge occur continuously. If yours is such a system, you should plan from the beginning to be able to quickly update the system as required. This process of updating your expert system is called "maintenance." Most software in regular use requires some maintenance to deal with changes that must be incorporated in order to protect the development investment.

If you have developed your system with a shell, changes should be easy to make. New rules can be written or existing rules modified. On the other hand, if you've used a programming language, maintenance can be far more difficult and time-consuming. New computer code may have to be written and integrated with existing code.

THE EXPERT SYSTEM DEVELOPMENT TEAM

The ideal development team comprises an expert, a knowledge engineer, and a programmer. The knowledge engineer is the link between the source of the knowledge and its storage in the computer, as shown in *Figure 7-1*. The knowledge engineer extracts the expert's knowledge and puts it into a suitable form. The programmer writes the code for putting the knowledge into memory and creates the inference engine and other components as required.

While this is probably the best development arrangement, it does require a great deal of cooperation and communication between the team members. A large system may require more members. The larger the team, then, the better the organization and management needed to create a workable system.

All projects may not require this ideal team. There are numerous variations. In some cases, the knowledge engineer and programmer will be the same person. An expert could also serve as the knowledge engineer after learning the process. Or a knowledge engineer could learn the domain. An efficient and cost-effective case finds one person playing all three roles.

If a shell is used, the programming aspect is eliminated and the knowledge engineer can easily learn to use the shell. In fact, since a shell essentially fixes the knowledge representation format and since shells are easy to use, an expert may be able to do the knowledge engineering.

**Figure 7-1.
Expert System
Development Team**

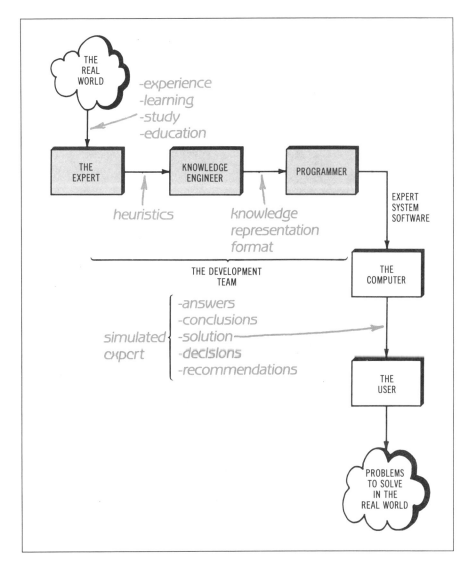

Be sure to consider some of these possibilities before initiating a development project. Find the optimum arrangement for you.

DEVELOPMENT PROCESS IN PERSPECTIVE

The development steps leading to an expert system are logical and easy to understand. Yet, the amount of work required to implement an expert system is unusually great. Most expert systems are very difficult, time-consuming, and expensive to develop. A simple, highly focused system built with available in-house expertise using a shell on a

PC might require six months to a year. But the very big systems often take years to perfect. The knowledge engineering takes the most time, but actual programming, if a shell is not used, also consumes a major amount of time and money. Once a prototype is built, testing and evaluation begin. The program eventually progresses through several stages before a final usable system evolves. Final testing in a real-world environment on genuine problems, perhaps involving additional changes, will take time. In general, few software development efforts are more complex than an expert system project. Don't make the mistake of underestimating the effort, cost, or time involved.

A DEVELOPMENT EXAMPLE

Induction System

To illustrate the steps we've described, let's look at a simple hypothetical example. This should give you a feel for what happens as the development progresses.

Step 1: Problem Definition

An electronic equipment manufacturer has discovered that many of its equipment problems can be traced to the power supply, the unit that converts the ac power-line voltage into the stable dc voltage that operates the circuits. Some power supplies have defects that occur during manufacturing. These must be found and corrected prior to shipping the equipment. Other units returned for repairs often have power-supply problems. These are corrected in a repair shop.

It usually takes a highly skilled technician to find these problems. The resulting repair is relatively easy and can be made by a less-skilled technician or even an assembler. There are only a few qualified technicians to do the actual troubleshooting, and they are already overloaded with work. Can this problem be solved with an expert system?

Step 2: Consider the alternatives

One choice is to hire more qualified technicians. This will solve the problem, but it is too expensive.

Another choice is to train new technicians. It would take a year or more of formal technician-level electronics training to bring others up to the expert level. Although willing candidates and a training budget are available, a faster solution is required to deal with the heavy backlog of repairs.

Documentation seems like a viable choice but existing manuals have not helped as the data they contain is hard to apply. There is no conventional software solution to this problem.

The decision is to create an expert system.

Step 3: Expert System Problem

Recall that a major category of expert systems is diagnosis and debugging. This is a perfect fit to this problem. We saw earlier that nine conditions must be met by a problem to consider an expert system as a viable solution:

1. Knowledge required to solve problem
2. Experts available
3. Narrow domain
4. Symbolic knowledge
5. High return on investment
6. No common sense needed
7. Moderate problem difficulty
8. Requires cognitive solution
9. Reasonable number of outcomes

Step 4: Estimate the Payoff

A quick calculation estimates a potential savings of $40,000 per year. One-time development costs are estimated to be about $25,000 using a shell. The payoff is high as productivity should increase measurably in both the manufacturing and repair departments. The return on investment looks good.

Step 5: Choose a Tool

Since no in-house programming expertise is available, a shell is selected as the development tool. An induction system for a PC is chosen to ease the development burden, as this is a first expert system project. The technicians are PC literate and, given time to learn the shell, should be able to create the expert system themselves with a little help from a systems analyst from the DP/MS department who will act as project coordinator and knowledge engineer.

Step 6: Knowledge Engineering

All the relevant printed data is collected first. This consists of a power-supply schematic diagram, a parts list, a circuit description from the technical manual, and some handwritten notes and tables the technicians use in keeping track of recurring troubles and selecting a fix.

Using this data, the knowledge engineering begins. First, the power-supply operation is reviewed and possible failures contemplated. *Figure 7-2* shows a schematic of the power supply with a description of its operation.

Figure 7-2.
Power Supply and Its
Operation

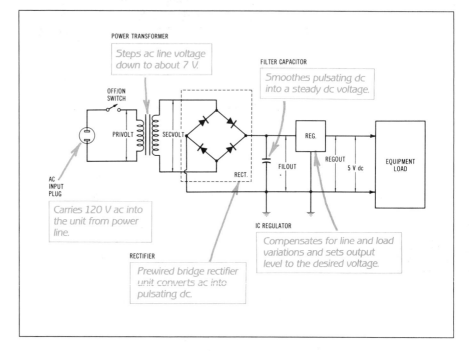

Next, a list of outcomes is made. Each of these is one of the components of the power supply that can fail:

1. Off-on switch (sw)
2. Transformer (xmfr)
3. Rectifier (rect)
4. Filter capacitor (cap)
5. Shorted regulator (shortreg)
6. Open regulator (openreg)

Note the abbreviations which will be used in entering data.

The regulator can fail two ways, so both are given. Once the bad part is identified, an assembler or junior technician can replace it, restoring proper operation.

The input data required by the system is now defined. To determine the status of the power supply, an assembler or junior technician makes voltage measurements at various points in the circuit. These voltages are labeled in *Figure 7-2* and listed below:

1. Regulator output voltage (regout)
2. Filter output or rectifier output (filout)
3. Transformer secondary winding voltage (secvolt)
4. Transformer primary winding voltage (privolt)

Again, note the shorthand abbreviations of these voltages. These will be used in entering facts into the shell.

Step 7: Build the Knowledge Base

Because our shell is the induction type, we must create some examples to put into a matrix. We go right to the heart of the matter by creating a matrix with our outcomes or results column containing the six conclusions listed earlier. The four voltage measurements from step 6 become our attributes columns. Now, with the help of our top technician serving as expert, we fill in the matrix with examples. We use such values as ok, low, high, norm (normal), and zero to indicate each attribute. The result looks like that in *Figure 7-3.*

**Figure 7-3.
Example Matrix for
Power-Supply Diagnosis**

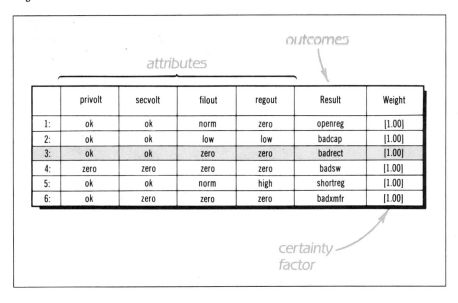

	privolt	secvolt	filout	regout	Result	Weight
1:	ok	ok	norm	zero	openreg	[1.00]
2:	ok	ok	low	low	badcap	[1.00]
3:	ok	ok	zero	zero	badrect	[1.00]
4:	zero	zero	zero	zero	badsw	[1.00]
5:	ok	ok	norm	high	shortreg	[1.00]
6:	ok	zero	zero	zero	badxmfr	[1.00]

The weight column is for recording a certainty factor based on a 0–1.0 scale. It designates how confident we are of the result. Here, all outcomes get a 1.0, meaning 100 percent.

Step 8: Develop the Software

Now we boot up the shell and transfer the matrix into it. The shell induces the rules, which are given in the form of a decision tree. *Figure 7-4* shows the tree induced by the commercial shell 1st Class.

**Figure 7-4.
Decision Tree for
Power-Supply Trouble**

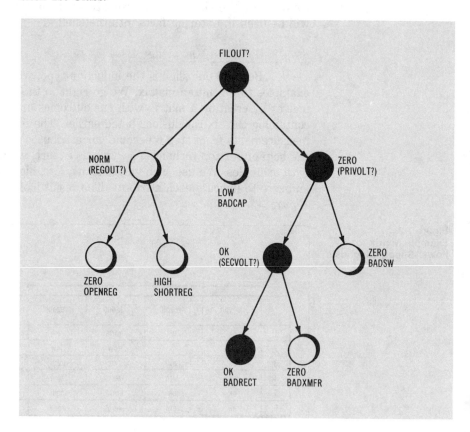

Each node represents some condition. Also, at some nodes a question is asked (in parentheses). The questions are those that will be asked by the system in order to gather data for a decision. The answers are the branch nodes. As each question is answered, a new path is selected. Eventually, the path ends in a conclusion.

Step 9: Test and Validate the System

The prototype system is next tested by all the technicians and on a representative group of assemblers and other less-skilled workers. The system works! A typical consultation with the system is now shown in *Figure 7-5*.

Figure 7-5.
Four Screens a User
Sees During Advisory
Session

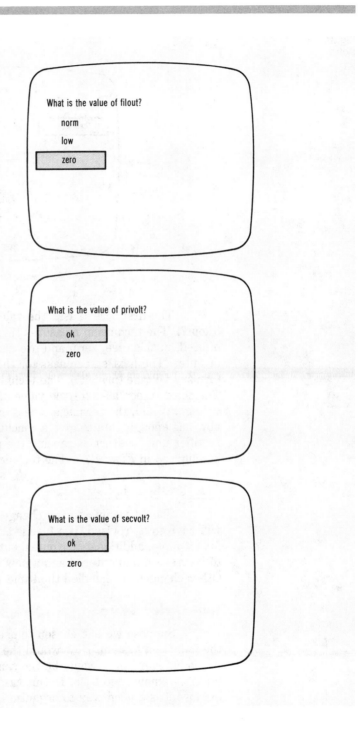

**Figure 7-5
Cont.**

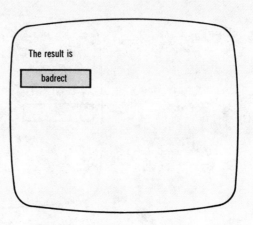

The first screen asks the value of the filter output voltage (filout?). The technician measures this; selects one of the choices offered, in this case, zero; and presses the key for carriage return or enter. The next screen asks for the value of the transformer primary voltage (privolt?). The technician selects the choice OK. The third screen asks for the value of the transformer secondary voltage. Again, the technician measures and selects OK. The system now has enough data to give a conclusion. In this case, a bad rectifier unit (badrect) is causing the problem. This path is highlighted in *Figure 7-3*. The technician can now make the repair.

Step 10: Maintain the System

Should manufacturing changes be made, the expert system will have to be revised. If a fuse is added to the secondary winding, for example, additional attributes, outcomes, and examples will have to be created and entered and a new decision tree will be inferred. Other changes are handled the same way.

Rule-Based System

Suppose we had chosen to use a rule-based shell instead of the induction system. How would the development be different? Actually, everything would be the same up to step 7, where we build the knowledge base. In this case, we would make a matrix because it is a good way to organize knowledge. However, we would have to write our own rules based on the matrix.

Step 7: Build the Knowledge Base Again—with Rules

A simple way to do this is to create one rule for each example in the matrix. Each attribute would be an IF/AND statement. Our rule base would look like this:

1. IF   privolt is OK
    AND   secvolt is OK
    AND   filout is norm
    AND   regout is zero.
    THEN the problem is openreg

2. IF   privolt is OK
    AND   secvolt is OK
    AND   filout is low
    AND   regout is low
    THEN the problem is badcap

3. IF   privolt is OK
    AND   secvolt is OK
    AND   filout is zero
    AND   regout is zero
    THEN the problem is badrect

4. IF   privolt is zero
    AND   secvolt is zero
    AND   filout is zero
    AND   regout is zero
    THEN the problem is badsw

5. IF   privolt is OK
    AND   secvolt is OK
    AND   filout is norm
    AND   regout is high
    THEN the problem is shortreg

6. IF   privolt is OK
    AND   secvolt is zero
    AND   filout is zero
    AND   regout is zero
    THEN the problem is badxmfr

Compare these rules to the matrix to see how they match up.

This is the brute-force way to write the rules. And it works. It is inefficient, however, because there are more IF/AND clauses than there need to be. This takes up extra memory space and makes the search take longer as more attributes have to be matched.

A more efficient way to write rules is to look for patterns among the attributes. Try sketching a tree that shows the various paths. Once you learn to spot patterns, you'll be able to create optimum trees like the one in *Figure 7-4*. This leads to a shorter, more concise, rule set.

1. IF   filout is norm
   AND   regout is zero
   THEN the problem is openreg

2. IF   filout is norm
   AND   regout is high
   THEN the problem is shortreg

3. IF   filout is low
   THEN the problem is badcap

4. IF   filout is zero
   AND   privolt is OK
   AND   secvolt is OK
   THEN the problem is badrect

5. IF   filout is zero
   AND   privolt is OK
   AND   secvolt is zero
   THEN the problem is badxmfr

6. IF   filout is zero
   AND   privolt is zero
   THEN the problem is badsw

You can write this rule base directly from *Figure 7-4*. Each node is a condition satisfying some outcome. There has to be one rule for each outcome. That's the absolute minimum number of rules in any expert system.

Now compare the second rule set with the brute-force set we first wrote. There are thirty IF/AND/THEN statements in the original set and only nineteen in this compact set. Less memory is used and the search will be much faster. In a big system, the performance difference can be enormous.

Now, how would a backward-chaining rule-based shell work with this rule base? Let's assume our problem is badrect as before.

First, the inference engine selects one of the outcomes. Assume it chooses openreg. Again we follow the path in *Figure 7-4*. The inference engine first searches for a rule that concludes openreg. It finds rule 1 in the optimized rule set. Now the inference engine has to prove this outcome. It does this by asking questions based on the AND and IF statements. "What is regout?" is the first question. With a bad rectifier, regout would be zero. So the user keys in zero. This satisfies the AND statement in rule 1. Next the system asks "what is filout?" With a bad rectifier, filout would be zero. This doesn't match the IF statement in rule 1. So that line of reasoning is abandoned.

The inference engine then selects the next outcome, shortreg. It looks at the THEN statements in the rule base and finds rule 2. Now seeking proof, it asks "what is regout?" With a bad rectifier, regout would be zero. That input doesn't satisfy rule 2 so the inference engine moves on.

Next, it picks up outcome badcap. It finds rule 3 with badcap in the THEN statement. It then asks a question based on the IF statement. "What is filout?" With a bad rectifier, filout would be zero. That doesn't match the IF statement. So rule 3 is also dropped.

The inference engine now picks up badrect. It finds this in the THEN statement of rule 4. To satisfy this rule, it asks for secvolt. We type in OK. That matches the second AND statement. Next, it asks for privolt. We respond with OK. That matches the first AND statement. The system then asks for filout. We give it zero. That too is a match in the IF statement. All conditions of the rule are satisfied, so rule 4 fires and the system concludes that the problem is a bad rectifier.

While this example was made trivial to aid in understanding expert system development and operation, it could be expanded into a practical and useful program. While we only covered the major components, it would be relatively easy to add other defects such as shorted load, open wires or cracked lands on the printed circuit board, or solder bridges. We would have to make additional measurements in order to provide sufficient data for decision-making. Nevertheless, the final program could quickly identify all the common problems. Further, we would want to add explanatory text to give additional helpful advice.

What Have We Learned?

1. Expert system development is a ten-step process. The first five steps cover initial planning, definition, and preparation. These include problem definition, alternative evaluation, determination of the suitability of the problem to an expert system, payoff estimation, and development tool selection.

2. Some alternatives to an expert system include hiring more experts, creating documentation and job aids, using conventional software, training and education.

3. Nine conditions must be met in order for an expert system to fit the defined problem: knowledge required to solve the problem, experts available, a narrow domain, symbolic knowledge, high payoff, common sense not required, moderate problem difficulty, a cognitive rather than physical solution, and a reasonable number of outcomes.

4. In order to justify an expert system, its development cost must be less than the savings, revenue, or benefits it generates.

5. In selecting a development tool, make a shell your first choice as it will greatly facilitate the project. Buy the largest and best shell within your budget even though you may not expect to use all its capability. If a shell is not available or the problem does not fit a shell, then an AI language such as Prolog or LISP should be your next choice. Only as a last resort should you use a conventional language.

6. The last five development steps are knowledge engineering, building the knowledge base, developing the software, testing and debugging, and maintaining.

7. The job of the knowledge engineer is to interview and observe the expert to extract his or her knowledge.

8. Building the knowledge base consists of organizing, formatting, and analyzing the knowledge so that it can be represented in rules or another structure. This process includes identifying outcomes and input data and creating an outline, tree, or matrix to help visualize the knowledge.

9. Developing the software involves entering the knowledge into the shell or writing code in the selected implementation language.

10. The system must be tested on experts and users to check its validity and to catch bugs.

11. Knowledge is dynamic in some domains and must be periodically updated to keep the expert system current.

Quiz for Chapter 7

1. Which of the following is *not* a potential alternative to an expert system?
   a. Training.
   b. Conventional software.
   c. Documentation.
   d. Employee relocation.

2. Which of the following conditions must be met in order for the problem to be suitable for an expert system solution?
   a. Narrow domain.
   b. Common sense required.
   c. Documentation sources available.
   d. Solution requires source of information.

3. If the development costs exceed the estimated benefits, then:
   a. development costs should be reduced.
   b. an expert system should not be developed.
   c. conventional software should be used.
   d. new benefits must be found.

4. The best tool for expert system development is:
   a. C.
   b. LISP.
   c. a shell.
   d. Prolog.

5. Personal computers are typically not capable of handling expert systems with more than:
   a. 200 rules.
   b. 400 rules.
   c. 500 rules.
   d. 1000 rules.

6. If a shell fits the problem but is not available for the host computer, a suitable alternative is the language:
   a. C.
   b. Pascal.
   c. LISP.
   d. Prolog.

7. The main limitations of personal computers in running large expert systems are:
   a. RAM size and CPU speed.
   b. RAM and disk size.
   c. CPU speed and disk size.
   d. clock speed and RAM access time.

8. Which of the following is most true about a shell?
   a. Don't buy any more shell than you need.
   b. Languages are better than shells.
   c. Buy the biggest and best shell you can afford.
   d. Rule-based shells are better than induction shells.

9. The development person responsible for organizing, managing, and guiding expert system development is the:
   a. expert.
   b. programmer.
   c. department manager.
   d. knowledge engineer.

10. Expert knowledge is obtained by:
    a. getting the expert to write a report.
    b. interviewing and observing an expert.
    c. reading the literature.
    d. surveying multiple experts.

11. Creating a knowledge base begins with:
    a. listing all possible outcomes.
    b. listing required data facts.
    c. drawing a decision tree.
    d. making a matrix.

12. An induction shell eliminates:
    a. matrix creation.
    b. rule writing.
    c. decision trees.
    d. the need for knowledge engineering.

13. A fast way to test and justify an expert system project is to:
    a. buy a shell.
    b. show a high return on investment.
    c. assemble a development team.
    d. develop a prototype.

14. To validate an expert system, it must be:
    a. tested on users.
    b. blessed by the experts.
    c. evaluated by programmers.
    d. sanctioned by management.

15. A shell is the preferred development tool in a dynamic domain because:
    a. execution speed is higher.
    b. less RAM is required.
    c. updating and maintenance is faster and easier.
    d. no knowledge engineer is needed.

Appendix: Vendors

EXPERT SYSTEM TOOLS

Abacus Programming Corp.
(ESI—$495)
14545 Victory Blvd.
Van Nuys, CA 91411

Artelligence, Inc. (OPS5+
—$3000; Prodigy—$450/950)
14902 Preston Rd., Suite 212-
252
Dallas, TX 75240

California Intelligence (XSYS—
$995)
912 Powell St., #8
San Francisco, CA 94108

Digitalk, Inc. (Methods—$79)
5200 West Century Blvd.
Los Angeles, CA 90045

Dynamic Master Systems, Inc.
(TOPSI—$175)
P. O. Box 566456
Atlanta, GA 30356

ExperTelligence, Inc.
(ExperOPS5—$325)
559 San Ysidro Rd.
Santa Barbara, CA 93108

Expert Systems, Inc. (Expert
Ease—$475)
868 West End Ave., Suite 3A
New York, NY 10025

Expert Systems International
(ES/P Advisor—$895)
1150 First Ave.
King of Prussia, PA 19439

EXSYS, Inc. (EXSYS—$295)
P. O. Box 75158
Contra Station
Albuquerque, NM 98194

General Research Corp. (TIMM
—$9500)
7655 Old Springhouse Rd.
McLean, VA 22102

Human Edge Software Corp.
(Expert Edge—$795; Expert
Ease—$475)
2445 Faber Place
Palo Alto, CA 94303

These prices are of course subject to change. We include them here to give you a
sense of the price range for commercial expert systems.

Inference Corp. (ART—Prices vary for different computers)
5300 W. Century Blvd.
Los Angeles, CA 90045

IntelligenceWare Inc. (Intelligence/Compiler 1.0a—$990)
9800 S. Sepulveda Blvd. Suite 730
Los Angeles, CA 90045

Intelligent Machine Co. (KNOWOL—$40; KNOWOL+—$100)
1907 Red Oak Circle
New Port Richie, FL 33553

KDS Corp. (KDS—$795; Playback—$495)
934 Hunter Rd.
Wilmette, IL 60091

Kemp-Carraway Heart Institute (FLOPS—$195)
Birmingham, AL 35234

Level Five Research Inc. (Insight—$95; Insight-2+—$485)
503 Fifth Ave.
Indialantic, FL 32903

Lightwave Consultants (ESIE—$145 [subset available in public domain])
P. O. Box 290539
Tampa, FL 33617

Micro Data Base Systems, Inc. (GURU—$2950)
P. O. Box 248
Lafayette, IN 47902

Mountain View Press, Inc. (Expert-2—$100)
P. O. Box 4656
Mountain View, CA 94040

Neuron Data, Inc. (Nexpert—$5000)
444 High St.
Palo Alto, CA 94301

Paperback Software, Inc. (VP-Expert—$100)
2830 Ninth St.
Berkeley, CA 94710

Potomac Pacific Engineering, Inc. (Expert System Tool—$20)
P. O. Box 2027
Gaithersburg, MD 20879

Production Systems Technologies, Inc. (OPS/83—$1950-$25,000)
642 Gettysburg St.
Pittsburgh, PA 15206

Programming Logic Systems, Inc. (Apes—$425)
31 Crescent Dr.
Milford, CT 06460

Programs in Motion, Inc. (1st Class—$495)
10 Sycamore Rd.
Wayland, MA 01778

Radian Corp. (Rule Master—$5000)
8501 Mo-Pac Blvd.
P. O. Box 9948
Austin, TX

Software A&E, Inc. (KES—
$4000)
1500 Wilson Blvd., Suite 800
Arlington, VA 22209

Software Intelligence
Laboratory, Inc. (WIZDOM—
$250)
1593 Locust Ave.
Bohemia, NY 11716

Software Plus (CxPERT—$165)
1652 Albermarle Dr.
Crofton, MD 21114

SRI International (SeRIES—
$5000)
333 Ravenswood Ave.
Menlo Park, CA 94301

Teknowledge Inc. (M 1—$5000)
525 University Ave., Suite 200
Palo Alto, CA 94301

Texas Instruments, Inc.
(Personal Consultant Plus—
$2950)
P. O. Box 809063
Dallas, TX 75380

Thinking Software, Inc. (Turbo
Expert/Level 1—$179, Level 2
—$359)
46-16 165th Place
Woodside, NY 11377

Ultimate Media, Inc. (Advisor
—$100)
275 Magnolia Ave.
Larkspur, CA 94939

Xerox (Humble—$299
[Smalltalk])
250 North Halstead St.
P. O. Box 7018
Pasadena, CA 91109

AI LANGUAGES

LISP

Automata Design Associates
(UNXLISP—$86)
1570 Arran Way
Dresher, PA 19025

CRIL (Le LISP—$3000)
12 Bis, Rue Jean-Jaures
92807 Puteaux, France

Cybermetrics (UNXLISP—$70)
P. O. Box 1194
Los Gatos, CA 95031

Digital Equipment Corp.
(GCLISP—$495; ISI-Interlisp—
$10,000)
146 Main St.
Manard, MA 61754

ExperTelligence, Inc.
(ExperLISP—$325)
559 San Ysidro Rd.
Santa Barbara, CA 93108

Franz, Inc. (Franz LISP—$995)
1141 Harbor Bay Parkway
Alameda, CA 94501

Gnosis, Inc. (P-LISP—$80)
4005 Chestnut St.
Philadelphia, PA 19104

Gold Hill Computers, Inc.
(GCLISP—$495)
163 Harvard St.
Cambridge, MA 02139

Integral Quality Inc. (IQLISP
—$175)
P. O. Box 31970
Seattle, WA 31970

IOTC (PC-LISP—$125)
P. O. Box 1365
Laramie, WY 87070

Levien Instrument (BYSO-
LISP—$150)
Box 31
McDowell, VA 24458

The LISP Company
(TLC__LISP 86—$169)
430 Monterey Ave., #4
Los Gatos, CA 95030

LUCID, Inc. (LUCID
CommonLISP—prices vary for
different computers)
707 Laurel St.
Menlo Park, CA 94025

Microsoft Inc. (MuLISP—$300)
10700 Northup Way
P. O. Box 97200
Bellevue, WA 98009

Norell Data Systems (LISP/88
—$50)
P. O. Box 70127
3400 Wilshire Blvd.
Los Angeles, CA 90010

Northwest Computer
Algorithms (UO-LISP—$150)
P. O. Box 90995
Bellevue, WA 98009

PC/BLUE Users Group
(XLISP—$7)
The New York Amateur
Computer Club Inc.
Box 106
Church Street Station
New York, NY 10008

Pro Code International (Waltz
LISP—$169)
15930 SW Colony Place
Portland, OR 97224

Software Toolworks (LISP/80—
$40)
15223 Ventura Blvd., Suite
1118
Sherman Oaks, CA 91403

Solution Systems (TransLISP—
$75)
335 - SL Washington St.
Norwell, MA 02061

System Designers Software
(PROLOG[LISP + Prolog]—
$1950)
5203 Leesburg Pike
Falls Church, VA 22041

Texas Instruments, Inc. (PC
Scheme—$95)
P. O. Box 809063
Dallas, TX 75380

University of Utah (Portable
Standard LISP—$750)
3160 MEB
Salt Lake City, UT 84112

Prolog

Arity Corp. (Arity/Prolog
Interpreter—$495; Compiler—
$1950)
358 Baker Ave.
Concord, MA 01742

Automata Design Associates
(Prolog—$30)
1570 Arran Way
Dresher, PA 19025

Borland International (Turbo
Prolog—$100)
4585 Scotts Valley Dr.
Scotts Valley, CA 95066

Chalcedony Software
(PROLOG V—$70)
6680 La Jolla Blvd.
Suite 126C
La Jolla, CA 92037

CRIL (Prolog/P—$400)
12 Bis, Rue Jean Jaures
92807 Puteaux, France

Expert Systems International
(PROLOG-1—$395; PROLOG-2
—$1895)
1150 First Ave.
King of Prussia, PA 19406

Interface Computer GmbH
(IF/Prolog—price unavailable)
Oberfoehringer Str. 24a
D-8000 Muenchen 81
West Germany

Logicware Inc. (MPROLOG—
$725)
20 William St., Suite 200
Wellesley, MA 02181

Programming Logic Systems
(LPA Prolog—$395;
MicroProlog APES—$395)
31 Crescent Dr.
Milford, CT 06460

Quintus Computer Systems
Inc. (Quintus Prolog—$79)
2345 Yale St.
Palo Alto, CA 94306

Solution Systems (Prolog-86—
$125)
335-L Washington St.
Norwell, MA 02061

Smalltalk and Others

Digitalk Inc. (Smalltalk—$100)
5200 W. Century Blvd.
Los Angeles, CA 90045

Productivity Products
International (Objective-C—
27 Glen Rd.
Sandy Hook, CT 06482

Softsmarts, Inc. (Smalltalk AT
—$205)
299 California Ave.
Palo Alto, CA 94306

Verac Inc. (GeoFlavors—
9605 Scranton Rd. Suite 500
San Diego, CA 92121

LISP MACHINES AND AI WORKSTATIONS

Hewlett-Packard Corp.
(Call the local office)

LISP Machines Inc.
6033 West Century Blvd.
Los Angeles, CA 90045

Unisys Corp.
(Call the local office)

Symbolics Inc.
11 Cambridge Center
Cambridge, MA 02142

Tektronix Inc.
P. O. Box 500, Mail Stop 63635
Beaverton, OR 97077

Texas Instruments
P. O. Box 225012, Mail Station 57
Dallas, TX 75265

Xerox Special Information Systems
250 North Halstead St.
Pasadena, CA 91109

AI SOFTWARE AND SERVICES

Abacus Programming Corp.
(Programming, consulting)
14545 Victory Blvd.
Van Nuys, CA 91411

Applied Expert Systems, Inc.
5 Cambridge Center
Cambridge, MA 02142

ArtelIgence, Inc. (Expert
system tools)
14902 Preston Rd.
#212-252
Dallas, TX 75240

Arthur Anderson
69 West Washington St.
Chicago, IL 60602

Arthur D. Little Inc.
Acorn Park
Cambridge, MA 02142

Artificial Intelligence Corp.
(Natural language processors)
100 Fifth Ave.
Waltham, MA 02254

Bolt, Beranek & Newman, Inc.
10 Moulton St.
Cambridge, MA 02338

Brattle Research Corp.
215 First St.
Cambridge, MA 02142

Carnegie Group Inc.
(Knowledge-base tools,
consulting)
650 Commerce Ct.
Station Sq.
Pittsburgh, PA 15219

Chalcedony Software (Prolog)
5580 La Jolla Blvd.
La Jolla, CA 92137

Cognitive Systems
234 Church St.
New Haven, CT 06510

Decision Support Software,
Inc.
1300 Vincent Pl.
McLean, VA 22101

ExperTelligence (LISP, LOGO,
expert system tools)
559 San Ysedro Rd.
Santa Barbara, CA 93108

Expert Knowledge Systems,
Inc. (Knowledge engineering,
consulting)
P. O. Box 6600
McLean, VA 22106

Expert Systems, Inc.
868 West End Ave., Suite 3A
New York, NY 10025

Expert Systems International
(Prolog, expert system tools)
1150 First St.
King of Prussia, PA 19406

EXSYS, Inc. (Expert systems
tools)
P. O. Box 75158, Contract
Station 14
Albuquerque, NM 87194

Franz, Inc. (LISP)
6321 Thornhill Dr.
Oakland, CA 94611

General Research Corp.
(Expert systems tools)
7655 Old Spring Rd.
McLean, VA 22102

Gold Hill Computers (LISP)
163 Harvard St.
Cambridge, MA 02139

Human Edge Software, Inc.
(Expert systems tools)
2445 Faber Pl.
Palo Alto, CA 94303

Inference Corp. (Expert
systems tools)
5300 W. Century Blvd. #501
Los Angeles, CA 90045

Infotym
20705 Valley Green Dr.
Cupertino, CA 95014

Intellicorp (Software tools)
707 Laurel St.
Menlo Park, CA 94025

Intermetrics (Software tools)
733 Concord Ave.
Cambridge, MA 02138

Jeffrey Perrone & Associates,
Inc. (Consulting)
3685 17th St.
San Francisco, CA 94114

Level 5 Research (Expert
systems tools)
503 Fifth Ave.
Indialantic, FL 32903

Logicware, Inc. (Prolog)
1000 Finch Ave. West
Toronto, Ontario Canada
M3J2V5

Palladian Software (Financial
expert systems)
14 Munroe St.
Cambridge, MA 02142

Radian Corp. (Consulting,
expert systems)
8501 Mo Pac Blvd.
Austin, TX 78766

Silogic Inc. (The Knowledge
WorkBench [software])
9841 Airport Blvd. Suite 600
Los Angeles, CA 90045

Smart Systems Technology
(Consulting, training)
6870 Elm St.
McLean, VA 22101

Solution Systems (Prolog &
LISP)
335 W. Washington St.
Norwell, MA 02001

SRI International (Research,
consulting, expert system tools)
333 Ravenswood
Menlo Park, CA 94025

Syntelligence, Inc.
1000 Hamlin Ct.
Sunnyvale, CA 94088

System Designers Software,
Inc. (Prolog, LISP)
5203 Leesburg Pike, Suite 1201
Falls Church, VA 22041

Teknowledge, Inc. (Expert
systems tools, consulting,
design)
525 University Ave.
Palo Alto, CA 94301

Teknowledgy Sources, Inc.
(Consulting)
11915 Latigo Lane
Oakton, VA 22124

Texas Instruments, Inc.
(Expert systems tools, LISP
machines)
12501 Research Blvd.
Austin, TX 78769

Bibliography

BOOKS ABOUT AI

Those books marked with an asterisk were most interesting and useful in researching this book.

Albus, James S. *Brains, Behavior & Robotics.* New York, NY: Byte/McGraw-Hill, 1981.

Aleksander, I. *Artificial Vision for Robots.* New York, NY: Chapman & Hall, 1983.

Androiole, Stephen J., ed. *Applications in Artificial Intelligence.** Princeton, NJ: Petrocelli Books, 1985.

Banerji, Ranan B. *Artificial Intelligence: A Theoretical Approach.* New York, NY: North Holland, 1980.

Barr, Avron, Edward A. Feigenbaum, and Paul Cohen. *The Handbook of Artificial Intelligence, Vols. I, II, and III.** Los Altos, CA: William Kaufmann, 1981.

Boden, Margaret. *Artificial Intelligence and Natural Man.* New York, NY: Basic Books, 1977.

Brownston, L., R. Farrell, E. Kant, and N. Martin. *Programming Expert Systems in OPS5: An Introduction to Rule-Based Programming.* Reading, MA: Addison-Wesley, 1985.

Buchanan, Bruce G. and Edward H. Shortliffe. *Rule-Based Expert Systems.* Reading, MA: Addison-Wesley, 1984.

Bundy, A. *Artificial Intelligence: An Introductory Course.* New York, NY: North Holland, 1978.

Bundy, Alan. *Catalogue of Artificial Intelligence Tools.* New York, NY: Springer-Verlag, 1984.

Charniak, E. and D. McDermott. *Introduction to Artificial Intelligence.* Reading, MA: Addison-Wesley, 1985.

Evans, C. *The Micro Millenium.* New York, NY: Viking Penguin, 1979.

Feigenbaum, Edward A. and Pamela McCorduck. Reading, MA: Addison-Wesley, 1981.

Forsyth, Richard and Chris Naylor. *The Hitch-Hiker's Guide to Artificial Intelligence.** New York, NY: Chapman & Hall, 1985.

Gloess, Paul Y. *Understanding Artificial Intelligence.* Sherman Oaks, CA: Alfred Publishing, 1981.

Graham, Neil. *Artificial Intelligence, Making Machines "Think."** Blue Ridge Summit, PA: TAB Books, 1979.

Harmon, Paul and David King. *Expert Systems.* New York, NY: Wiley, 1984.

Harris, Mary Dee. *Introduction to Natural Language Processing.* Reston, VA: Reston, 1985.

Hayes, J. E. and D. Michie. *Intelligent Systems.* New York, NY: Halsted Press, 1983.

Hayes-Roth, Frederick, Donald A. Waterman and Douglas B. Lenat. *Building Expert Systems.* Reading, MA: Addison-Wesley, 1983.

Hofstadter, Douglas R. *Godel, Escher, Bach: An Eternal Golden Brain.* New York, NY: Vintage Books, 1980.

Information Industry Association. *Artificial Intelligence: Reality or Fantasy?* 1984.

Jenkins, Richard A. *Supercomputers of Today and Tomorrow: The Parallel Processing Revolution.* Blue Ridge Summit, PA: TAB Books, 1986.

Krutch, John. *Experiments in Artificial Intelligence.* Indianapolis, IN: Howard W. Sams, 1981.

Marr, David. *VISION.* New York, NY: W. H. Freeman, 1982.

McCorduck, Pamela. *Machines Who Think.* New York, NY: W. H. Freeman, 1979.

Mischkoff, Henry C. *Understanding Artificial Intelligence.* Indianapolis, IN: Howard W. Sams, 1985.

Nagy, Tom, Dick Gault, and Monica Nagy. *Building Your First Expert System.* Torrance, CA: Ashton Tate, 1985.

Naylor, Chris. *Build Your Own Expert System.* New York, NY: Halstead Press, 1983.

Nilsson, Nils J. *Principles of Artificial Intelligence.* Los Altos, CA: Tioga Publishing, 1980.

O'Malley, T. J. *Artificial Intelligence Projects for the Commodore 64.* Blue Ridge Summit, PA: TAB Books, 1985.

O'Shea, Tim and Mark Eisenstadt. *Artificial Intelligence: Tools, Techniques and Applications.* New York, NY: Harper & Row, 1985.

Peat, F. David. *Artificial Intelligence: How Machines Think.* New York, NY: Baen Publishing, 1985.

Rich, Elaine. *Artificial Intelligence.** New York, NY: McGraw-Hill, 1983.

Ritchie, David. *The Binary Brain: Artificial Intelligence in the Age of Electronics.* Reading, MA: Addison-Wesley, 1983.

Rose, Frank. *Into the Heart of Mind.* New York, NY: Harper & Row, 1984.

Schank, Roger C. and Peter G. Childers. *The Cognitive Computer.* Reading, MA: Addison-Wesley, 1984.

Shirai, Yoshiaki and Jun-ichi Tsujii. *Artificial Intelligence Concepts, Techniques & Applications.* New York, NY: Wiley, 1984.

Simon, Herbert A. *The Science of the Artificial.* Cambridge, MA: MIT Press, 1981.

Stevens, Lawrence. *Artificial Intelligence: The Search for the Perfect Machine.* Hasbrouck Heights, NJ: Hayden, 1985.

Thompson, Beverly and William. *Designing and Implementing Your Own Expert System.* New York, NY: Byte/McGraw-Hill, 1985.

Torrero, Edward A. *Next Generation Computer.* New York, NY: IEEE Press, 1986.

Townsend, Carl and Dennis Foucht. *Designing and Programming Personal Expert Systems.* Blue Ridge Summit, PA: TAB Books, 1986.

Waterman, Donald A. *A Guide to Expert Systems.** Reading, MA: Addison-Wesley, 1985.

Weiss, S. M. and C. A. Kulikowski. *A Practical Guide to Designing Expert Systems.* Totowa, NJ: Rowman & Allanheld, 1984.

Williamson, Mickey. *Artificial Intelligence for Microcomputers.* Bowie, MD: Brady Communications, 1986.

Winston, Patrick Henry. *Artificial Intelligence.* * Reading, MA: Addison-Wesley, 1984.

Winston, Patrick H. and Richard H. Brown. *Artificial Intelligence: An MIT Perspective, Vols. I & II.* Cambridge, MA: MIT Press, 1979.

Winston, Patrick H. and Karen A. Prendergast. *The AI Business.* Cambridge, MA: MIT Press, 1984.

BOOKS ABOUT AI LANGUAGES

LISP

Gloess, Paul Y. *Understanding LISP.* Sherman Oaks, CA: Alfred Publishing, 1982.

Gnosis. *Learning LISP.* Englewood Cliffs, NJ: Prentice-Hall, 1984.

Hasemer, Tony. *Looking at LISP.* Reading, MA: Addison-Wesley, 1984.

Steele, Guy L., Jr. *Common LISP.* Bedford, MA: Digital Press, 1984.

Touretzky, David S. *LISP—A Gentle Introduction to Symbolic Computing.* * New York, NY: Harper & Row, 1984.

Wilensky, Robert. *LISP Craft.* New York, NY: W. W. Norton, 1984.

Winston, P. O. and B. K. P. Horn. *LISP.* * Reading, MA: Addison-Wesley, 1984.

Prolog

Campbell, J. S., ed. *Implementations of Prolog.* Ellis Norwood Ltd., 1984.

Clark, K. L. and S. A. Tarnlund. *Logic Programming.* Orlando, FL: Academic Press, 1982.

Clocksin, W. F. and C. S. Mellish. *Programming in Prolog.* * New York, NY: Springer-Verlag, 1981.

Ennals, Richard. *Beginning Micro-Prolog.* New York, NY: Harper & Row, 1984.

Kowalski, R. *Logic for Problem Solving.* New York, NY: North Holland, 1979.

Lloyd, J. W. *Foundations of Logic Programming.* New York, NY: Springer-Verlag, 1984.

PUBLICATIONS ON AI AND EXPERT SYSTEMS

AI Expert
2443 Filmore St.
Suite 500
San Francisco, CA
94115

AI Magazine (quarterly)
American Association for Artificial Intelligence
445 Burgess Dr.
Menlo Park, CA
94025

AI Trends Newsletter
DM Data Inc.
6900 East Camelback Rd.
Scottsdale, AZ 85251

Applied Artificial Intelligence Reporter (monthly)
ICS—University of Miami
P. O. Box 248235
Coral Gables, FL
33124

Artificial Intelligence Markets
AIM Publications Inc.
P. O. Box 156
Natick, MA
01760

Artificial Intelligence Report
Booz-Allen & Hamilton
4330 East-West Highway
Bethesda, MD 20814

The Artificial Intelligence Report
SRI International
3600 West Bayshore Rd.
Palo Alto, CA
94303

Expert Systems Journal
Learned Information
Besselsleigh Rd.
Abingdon, Oxford
OX136LG U.K.

Expert System Strategies
Cutter Information Corp.
1100 Massachusetts Ave.
Arlington, MA
02174-9990

Expert System User Magazine
Cromwell House
20 Bride Lane
London EC48DX U.K.

IEEE Expert (quarterly)
345 East 47th St.
New York, NY 10017

Intelligence
P. O. Box 20008
New York, NY 10025

International Journal of Intelligent Systems
John Wiley & Sons Inc.
605 Third Ave.
New York, NY 10158

Journal of Automated Reasoning
Kluwer Academic Publishers
101 Philip Dr.
Norwell, MA
02061

Knowledge Engineering
Richmond Research
Box 366, Village Station
201 Varick St.
New York, NY 10014

Release 1.0
Ziff-Davis Publishing Co.
One Park Ave.
New York, NY
10016

PC AI
3310 West Bell Rd.
Suite 119
Phoenix, AZ
85023

The Spang Robinson Report
3600 West Bayshore Rd.
Palo Alto, CA
94303

Conferences, Seminars, Workshops, and Courses

The ATHENA Group
575 Madison Ave.
Suite 1006
New York, NY 10022

Continuing Education Institute
10889 Wilshire Blvd.
Los Angeles, CA 90024

Gartner Group
72 Cummings Point Rd.
Stamford, CT 06904

George Washington University
Continuing Engineering
Education
Washington, D. C. 20052

Harmon Associates
151 Collingwood
San Francisco, CA 94114

The Institute of Artificial
Intelligence
1888 Century Park East, Suite
1207
Los Angeles, CA 90067

Integrated Computer Syustems
6305 Arizona Pl.
P. O. Box 45405
Los Angeles, CA 90045

International Joint Conference
on Artificial Intelligence
A A A I
445 Burgess Dr.
Menlo Park, CA 94025

Massachusetts Institute of
Technology
Center for Advanced
Engineering Study
MIT Video Course
77 Massachusetts Ave., Room
9-234
Cambridge, MA 02139

McDonnell Douglas Knowledge
Engineering
Mail Stop VG2-B01
20705 Valley Green Dr.
Cupertino, CA 95014

Mystech Associates Inc.
Mark Center Office Park #14
1900 N. Beauregard St.
Alexandria, VA 22311

Purdue University
Division of Conferences
Stewart Center
West Lafayette, IN 47907

Smart Systems Technology
6870 Elm St.
McLean, VA 22101

Software Architecture and
Engineering Inc.
1500 Wilson Blvd., #800
Arlington, VA 22209

Sperry Corp.
P. O. Box 2191
Princeton, NJ 08543

Technology Transfer Institute
741 10th St.
Santa Monica, CA 90402

Tower Conference
Management Co.
331 West Wesley St.
Wheaton, IL 60187

U. S. Professional
Development Institute
1620 Elton Rd.
Silver Spring, MD 20903

Yourdon Inc.
1133 Avenue of the Americas
New York, NY 10036

Glossary

Algorithm: A step-by-step procedure for solving a problem. A precisely defined group of rules or processes that leads to a desired output from a given set of inputs.

AND/OR Tree: A form of graph or goal tree using the logical AND and OR functions that shows how goals and subgoals of a problem-solving process are related. A method of representing the solution of a problem that can be solved by breaking it up into a set of smaller problems.

Arc: The lines interconnecting nodes in a search tree or transition net.

Architecture: The structure, framework, or organization of a computer or of a program.

Argument: The independent variable of a function. A variable whose quantity determines the value of a function. The variables that appear in parentheses after a function or predicate name.

Array: A set, group, or series of numbers, terms, or elements arranged in a logical or meaningful pattern. A typical array might be a set of numbers arranged in rows and columns to form a matrix. (See also "Matrix.")

Artificial Intelligence (AI): The branch of computer science devoted to the study of how computers can be used to simulate or duplicate functions of the human brain. Hardware and software techniques that make it appear as though a computer is thinking, reasoning, making decisions, storing or retrieving knowledge, solving problems, and learning.

Atom: A symbol, group of symbols, or word used to represent numbers and non-numeric objects. The smallest element used to represent values or name objects in the LISP programming language. Multiple atoms, when combined, form lists.

Automatic Programming: The process by which a computer uses a special AI program to create another program to solve a problem. A technique that combines problem-solving techniques and a data base of task and programming knowledge to allow individuals to solve problems on a computer without having to write the programs themselves. The user describes the program and the computer generates the algorithm and then a program to solve the problem.

Backtracking: A technique used in tree searches. The process of working backwards from a failed objective or an incorrect result to examine unexplored alternatives. Simply the process of backing up to a previous choice point in a computation and trying again.

Backward-Chaining: A method of reasoning that starts with the desired goal and works backward, looking for facts and rules that support the desired outcome. A technique used in tree searches where a conclusion or objective is hypothesized and the system works backward to find rules that support the hypothesis. Also known as "goal-driven," "expectations-driven," or "top-down reasoning." Also called "backward-reasoning."

Blackboard: A method of organizing, presenting, and communicating information. A data structure made up of all of the hypotheses generated by the system. A central communications point for various knowledge sources in an intelligence system. These multiple sources of knowledge communicate through the blackboard, which is a common structure that contains the current status of the problem's solution.

Blind Search: A general category of search technique that makes use of no knowledge or heuristics to help accelerate or simplify the search process. A time-consuming and arbitrary search process that attempts to exhaust all possibilities in searching rather than rely upon information that can help narrow the search.

Bottom Up: A method of reasoning, searching, or parsing that starts with an initial state in a tree or the string to be parsed and works toward the goal or solution. A data-driven approach. (See "Forward-Chaining.")

Breadth-First: A search strategy in which all of the nodes on one level of the search tree are examined before any of the nodes of the next lower level.

C: A popular higher-level programming language widely used in systems and applications programming. Originally developed at AT&T's Bell Labs along with the UNIX operating system.

CAE: Acronym for computer-aided engineering. The use of the computer to aid in all engineering activities, including design, sometimes using AI techniques.

CAI: Acronym for computer-aided (or -assisted) instruction. Using a computer to teach.

CBT: Acronym for computer-based training. (See "CAI.")

Certainty Factor: A number assigned to a fact, action, or relationship that indicates how likely it is to be true or to happen. A certainty factor of 1.0 means 100 percent true, 0.5 means partially true, and 0.0 means not true. (See also "Confidence Factor.")

Children: Successor nodes to a parent node.

Closed-World Assumption: A kind of default reasoning in which the system assumes that if it has not been told that a particular fact is true, it assumes it to be false. All relationships not directly stated to be true are assumed to be not true.

Cognition: The process of knowing.

Cognitive Model: A computer model of human thinking. Theories derived from psychology of the human thought process which are developed into processes that can be implemented as intelligent computer programs.

Combinatorial Explosion: A condition or phenomena that occurs when attempting to solve large complex problems using search techniques. The condition that occurs when a large number of possible alternatives or sequences must be evaluated to find the optimum path to a solution or goal. The possibilities examined become too large and time-consuming, thereby making them impractical for computer implementation even on large, fast systems.

Common LISP: A popular dialect of the AI programming language LISP. An attempt to agree on a common subset of LISP primitives that can be widely supported and used for the purpose of encouraging greater portability of LISP programs.

Common Sense: The large, general, partly experiential base of knowledge that humans possess about the way things are and how they work.

Common Sense Reasoning: A kind of decision-making that permits the system to retract a conclusion in the face of new evidence. Also, the ability of a system to revise its decisions in light of new knowledge received or otherwise derived.

Computer Vision: A field of AI study that seeks to duplicate human vision for use in robots or other applications. Using a TV camera or optical sensors to "see," then converting their electrical output to binary signals that can be processed by the computer for the comparison, identification, and pattern-matching of input symbols or images.

Confidence Factor: A number or system of numbers indicating the certainty or confidence we have in a specific fact, statement, or piece of evidence. The degree of belief we have in our information or knowledge. A method of dealing with uncertainty in production-rule systems. Not the same as probability.

Conflict Resolution: The priority-ordering process an inferencing system uses to decide which rule to recognize or fire when more than one rule's IF statement(s) matches the data base.

Consultation System: A general term for expert and knowledge-based systems.

Control Strategy: A method of reasoning in a search space (i.e., forward- or backward-chaining, depth- or breadth-first, etc.).

CPU: Acronym for central processing unit. The heart of all digital computers that carries out most of the processing functions. A combination of the arithmetic logic unit (ALU) and the control section of a digital computer. A microprocessor.

Data Driven: A kind of inference used in tree searches. Data-directed reasoning is bottom-up or forward-chaining.

DBMS: Acronym for data base management systems. A form of general-purpose computer applications program used for the storage, organization, search, manipulation, and retrieval of information stored in various records and files.

Decision-Making Software: Programs using decision-theory algorithms to help humans make decisions in complex situations.

Decision-Support System: A class of software used by management to help make decisions. Software used for creating mathematical models of problems to be solved, usually incorporating a spreadsheet and often using AI techniques.

Decision Tree: A graphical structure of nodes and arcs that shows alternative paths for various decisions or outcomes.

Deduction: Coming to a conclusion by the process of reasoning. Reaching a decision through a rational or logical thought process.

Deductive Reasoning: In logic, reasoning from the general to the specific. Conclusions follow premises. Also called "consequent reasoning."

Default Reasoning: A process used to overcome the problem of insufficient information or knowledge. Default reasoning uses guesses and assumptions to reach goals or decisions. Unless the system has knowledge to the contrary, these defaults are assumed to be true and will be used in determining the outcome.

Default Value: A value automatically given to a symbol or variable if no other value is defined by the programmer or user.

DENDRAL: One of the first rule-based expert systems. A system used to determine the structure of an organic chemical compound using data acquired from mass spectrometers and nuclear magnetic resonance instruments.

Dependencies: How outcomes and decisions are related to and derived from prior knowledge and decisions.

Dependency-Directed Backtracking: A technique used in tree searches to accelerate and simplify the process of reaching a conclusion. The process of going back to and withdrawing only those decisions that lead to the incorrect outcome.

Depth-First: A search procedure that explores each branch of a search tree to its full vertical length from left to right. An arbitrary search technique used when there is no heuristic or other guiding information to help limit the search. Each branch is searched for a solution and if none is found, a new vertical branch is searched to its depth, and so on.

Domain: A field of knowledge or expertise. A problem area of interest in an AI application.

EL: An expert system for analyzing and understanding electronic circuits.

Embedded System: AI software built into or buried in and referenced by another larger piece of algorithmic software.

EMYCIN: An empty version of the widely known MYCIN expert system. The rules specific to MYCIN are removed, leaving a shell, a reasoning system, and a natural language interface. By adding rules for a different problem domain, EMYCIN permits the rapid implementation of new expert systems.

Environment: A software development facility usually including a programming language such as LISP and other utilities or programs to make software creation faster and easier.

Examples: A system of attributes and outcomes arranged in a matrix and used to capture and represent certain kinds of knowledge in an expert system. Production rules are usually inferred from the examples.

Expert System: A major class of artificial intelligence software. A program consisting of a knowledge base, an inference engine or reasoning system, and a natural language user interface. The expert system embodies all of the facts, information, knowledge, and rules of thumb and other elements of heuristic expertise in a specific domain. A user may tap this expertise as an expert advisor or a consultant to solve problems or make decisions.

Expert System Generator: A software tool designed to simplify the development of an expert system. Any program that permits the creation of an expert system without having to program all elements of it from scratch.

Facet: A feature or attribute associated with an object in a frame. (See also "Slot.")

Fifth Generation: The next phase or level of development of computers. The expression used by the Japanese to refer to their program designed to achieve supremacy in the computer business. A class of knowledge-based computers employing super high speed/parallel techniques and artificial intelligence.

Fire: To put into use one of the rules in a production system or knowledge-based system. To initiate the action specified by a rule if certain conditions are met. (See also "trigger.")

FLAVORS: An object-oriented programming language based on Smalltalk and used in some LISP machines.

FLOPS: Acronym for floating point operations per second. A term used to measure the performance of supercomputers and array processors that use floating point numbers. The usual measure is megaFLOPS or MFLOPS (millions of floating point operations per second).

Forward-Chaining: A problem-solving technique used in production and rule-based systems in which conclusions are drawn or decisions are made by starting with the known facts. A search procedure or reasoning process using known facts to produce new facts and to reach a final conclusion. Also known as "data-driven" or "bottom-up reasoning" and "inductive" or "antecedent reasoning."

Frame: A method of representing knowledge. An organization or collection of attributes, characteristics, or properties called "slots" that describe a particular object, event, or action. An outline or an hierarchical structure containing slots for listing relevant facts and attributes.

Front-End: A program or piece of hardware or both that serves as an interface between human and machine or program to accelerate or simplify usage.

Function: A mathematical expression or rule showing the correspondence between two sets such that there is a unique part in one set assigned to each part in the other. The relationship or association between one item from a set with each item of another set.

Fuzzy Reasoning: A method of dealing with inexact or imprecise information by making it of some value in determining an outcome. Techniques of avoiding complexities when dealing with subjective information or poorly understood processes. A method of determining an adequate solution from imprecise information.

Garbage Collection: In the LISP programming language (and some other languages), the process of gathering and eliminating unneeded, unwanted or, discarded data so as to create more memory space for further computation.

Goal Driven: A method of reasoning that begins with the goal or a conclusion and works backward through the rules and facts of a knowledge base searching for the path that will achieve the desired goal. (See also "Backward-Chaining.")

Granularity: A measure of how finely programs, information, or knowledge are subdivided.

Heuristic: Anything that helps a human or computer to discover or learn. The use of empirical knowledge to aid in problem-solving. Rules of thumb, tricks, procedural tips, and other information that help to guide, limit, and speed up the search process.

Hierarchy: A ranked or graded series of persons or things. A body of knowledge or information organized into successive ranks or grades. Most hierarchies can be illustrated with the use of tree graphs.

Hypothesis: A statement that is subject to proof or verification. A proposition used as the basis for argument, discussion, or reasoning. An assumption used as the basis for action.

ICAI: Acronym for intelligent computer-aided instruction. Using AI techniques in a special program used for teaching with a computer.

IF-THEN: The form of the rules used in many AI systems and programs and expert systems. A conditional rule in which a certain action is taken only if some condition is satisfied. Decision-making tests that initiate an action if a specific condition is met (i.e., IF it is dark outside, THEN turn the light on).

Induction Shell: A shell allows building an expert system by entering knowledge as examples in a matrix. The shell induces rules that are used in reasoning.

Inductive Reasoning: In logic, reasoning from the specific to the general. Also known as "conditional" or "antecedent reasoning."

Inference: The process of drawing a conclusion from given evidence. To reach a decision by reasoning.

Inference Engine: That part of an expert system that actually performs the reasoning function. That part of an AI program that analyzes the information or knowledge base using rules to make decisions or reach conclusions.

Inheritance: The process by which one object takes on or is assigned the characteristics of another object higher up in a hierarchy.

Instantiation: The process of assigning a specific value or name to a variable in a logic expression, making it a particular instance of that variable.

Instruction: A computer word or number that tells a computer CPU a specific thing to do. A statement or command in a program that specifies a unique action to be taken.

Intelligence: The ability to acquire and apply knowledge through thought and reason.

Interface: That portion of a computer system or program that links two other portions of the system and allows them to communicate. A portion of a computer program that interacts with both the computer user and the remainder of the program or system. A go-between.

InterLISP: A dialect of the LISP programming language implemented on Xerox AI workstations.

KIPS: Acronym for knowledge information processing system. The term often given to fifth generation computers.

Knowledge: Understanding, awareness, or familiarity acquired through education or experience. Anything that has been learned, perceived, discovered, inferred, and understood.

Knowledge Base: A collection of data, rules, inferences, and procedures organized into frames, blackboards, semantic networks, scripts, rules, and other formats. The assembly of all of the information and knowledge of a specific field of interest that forms the basis for an intelligent computer system.

Knowledge-Based Systems: AI programs that use a knowledge base as their source for problem-solving in a particular field of interest but do not use heuristics.

Knowledge Engineer: A person who designs and builds expert systems. Computer science/AI specialists who acquire knowledge from all sources including human experts and organize it into a knowledge base.

Knowledge Engineering: The process of acquiring and formatting knowledge to form a knowledge base.

Knowledge Representation: A vocabulary and syntax of symbols and conventions used to describe and present knowledge and information. The structure and organization of information used to solve a problem.

Knowledge Source: A body of knowledge in a specific domain relevant to solving specific classes of problems. Information that has been collected and codified and made applicable for use in an expert system.

Leaf: A node having no successor.

Learning: Gaining knowledge, understanding, or skill through education or experience. The process of improving performance by acquiring new knowledge.

LIPS: Acronym for logical inferences per second. The unit of measurement of processing speed for AI and fifth generation computers.

LISP: Acronym for ListProcessor. The most widely used AI programming language. Invented by John McCarthy at MIT in the late 1950s.

LISP Machine: A special-purpose digital computer or workstation with the LISP programming language is resident for AI program development.

List: A linear sequence of elements or objects separated by blank spaces and surrounded by parentheses. An arrangement of numbers, words, or other segments including atoms or other lists. The basic form of knowledge representation in the LISP programming language.

Logic: A system of reasoning based on the study of propositions and their analysis in making deductions. A system developed by philosophers and mathematicians for the process of making inferences from facts.

LOGO: A programming language incorporating LISP and artificial intelligence concepts. Developed by Seymour Papert at MIT, LOGO is designed for educational applications and to help people learn about programming and feedback.

LOOPS: A multielement programming language with rule-based, object-based, and logic-based segments. Used on Xerox AI workstations.

MACSYMA: An expert system used to help people solve complex applied mathematics problems. Provides fast, automatic solutions without problem-solving or programming. Excellent at algebraic simplification and integration. Also works with vectors, inequalities, series, and other mathematical forms.

Matrix: A grid of rows and columns forming cells into which symbolic data is entered. (See also "Array.")

Menu: A list of items displayed on a computer screen for user selection. A user-friendly approach to presenting control alternatives to a user rather than have the user remember specific commands or directives that must be typed in.

Meta: A prefix of a term that designates a self-reference to the given term. Several examples are given below.

Meta Cognition: Thinking about your own thought processes.

Meta Knowledge: Knowledge about knowledge.

Meta Rule: A rule that describes how rules should be used.

MIPS: Acronym for millions of instructions per second. A unit of measurement for determining the speed performance of a computer.

Monotonic Logic: A reasoning system based on rules or theorems that do not change as new rules are added or as new information is received. What is true remains true despite additions and other modifications.

MYCIN: One of the earliest practical expert systems. A rule-based, backward-chaining expert system that helps a doctor determine the probable identity of an infection and helps to prescribe appropriate treatment.

Natural Language: A language such as English used by humans in everyday conversation, reading, and writing.

Natural Language Interface: That portion of an expert system or other AI program that allows the user to communicate with the computer using the natural language. The interface understands and interprets natural language input and generates natural language outputs.

Natural Language Processing: Getting a computer to understand natural language as language rather than as a meaningless list of letters, words, or sounds. The process of extracting meaning from a natural language input.

Nodes: Places, goals, or subgoals in a search tree. Achievable states in a state space.

Nonmonotonic Logic: Reasoning based on rules or theorems that can change based on new input information. A kind of default reasoning.

Object-Oriented Programming: The use of statements and procedures called objects to represent knowledge and their use in writing programs by passing messages. The Smalltalk and FLAVORS languages are examples.

Operating System: The master control program for a computer. A collection of programs that allows the user to conveniently manipulate all facilities of the computer and to access and use various applications programs, languages, and utilities. A system for creating and maintaining computer files and automatically handling input/output routines for peripheral equipment.

OPS: A rule-based programming language used to develop expert systems and other AI programs at Carnegie-Mellon University. The best-known version is OPS5.

Paradigm: An example or model.

Parallel Architecture: New methods of creating computers that will operate faster. The use of multiple CPUs or other circuits to carry out simultaneous processing of multiple programs or different parts of one program in order to enhance performance. Computer designs that are essential to improving performance in AI applications.

Parsing: The process of breaking down a character string of natural language or computer language input into its component parts so that it can be more readily analyzed, interpreted, or understood. Examining natural language or computer language input to determine the function of the words or commands in the string in order to decide what action to take.

Path: A route or course through a search tree.

Pattern: A diagram, plan, model, or template to be followed or identified.

Pattern-Matching: The automatic recognition or identification of figures, characters, shapes, and forms according to predetermined conditions or standards. Usually the comparison of the pattern input to a stored template or standard that determines the closeness of fit.

Planning Systems: A form of AI program that helps to determine an optimum plan to reach a given goal. A computer program that analyzes the steps to be taken to reach a given goal and attempts to specify a sequence that will lead to the successful achievement of the objective. Used for determining priorities, setting schedules, resolving time conflicts, and so on.

Predicate: A statement about the subject of a proposition. An assertion that denotes the relationship among two or more objects or elements.

Predicate Calculus: A formal language or logic system used to express statements about objects in a domain and their relationships. A logical system that includes a rule of inference that states how symbols can be used to create a formula and how new formulas can be reduced or derived from the old formula. A system of reasoning widely used in AI programs to indicate relationships among data items.

Primitive: A fixed or built-in function or procedure in the LISP language.

Probability: A number indicating the likelihood of the occurrence of a specific event. A ratio of the number of expected occurrences to the number of repetitions required to achieve the expected occurrences. Often expressed as a percentage. Used in production systems to deal with uncertainty. Not a confidence factor.

Problem-Solving: What most AI programs do, includes the process of answering a question, seeking a solution to a tough issue, resolving a conflict, and making a decision.

Procedure: A way of doing something. In LISP, a statement that describes a specific computational process. (See also "Function.")

Production Rule: An IF-THEN rule. (See also "Rule.")

Production System: An AI problem-solving program consisting of a set of rules, a data base to which the rules are applied, and a control strategy for using the rules on the data base. A rule-based problem-solving system that typically uses a search process.

Program: A sequence of computer instructions or commands that implement an algorithm to solve a problem, perform a calculation or control function. (See also "Software.")

Prolog: Acronym for *Programming* in *Logic*. A popular AI programming language developed in France and based on the concept of predicate calculus.

Propositional Calculus: A form of logic system used for reasoning in which conclusions are drawn from a series of statements according to a set of rules.

PROSPECTOR: An expert system that helps find ore deposits from geological input data.

Pruning: Various techniques used to limit the search through a knowledge base or search tree.

R1: An expert system used to configure VAX computers. See "XCON."

Real-Time Computing: Processing that occurs fast enough to appear simultaneous or to keep up with other actions or operations.

Reasoning: The mental process of drawing conclusions from facts, observations, or hypotheses. Making inferences from arguments or evidence.

Recursive: Any operation that is defined in terms of itself. A technique for performing a repetitive operation in which the result of one repetition is usually dependent upon the result of a previous repetition. A self-referencing or self-modifying function or computer program.

Resolution: A method of deduction or theorem-proving used in predicate calculus to draw a conclusion from a set of premises. Also a measure of fineness of detail as in a video camera or CRT.

Robotics: The science of developing and using robots. Capable of performing human tasks, robots are mechanical devices usually under the control of a computer that are used for automating some manufacturing function. AI techniques are widely used to make robots intelligent.

Root Node: A node in a search tree with no predecessor. The starting node in a search tree.

Rule: A regulation or statement defining a particular conduct, habit, or behavior. In AI, a two-part direction consisting of a condition and a consequent action. An IF-THEN rule states that if a given condition is true, then a specific action should be taken.

Rule-Based: Any program or system that uses a set of rules to draw conclusions, make decisions, and solve problems.

Rule of Thumb: A heuristic. A principle, technique, trick, or method often used to simplify, accelerate, or otherwise facilitate a process. A technique that does not always work or that is not always accurate. A general guideline.

Run-Time System: A piece of software that enables a user to run a program created with a software package but not to develop or modify programs.

Scenario: A summary or outline of a plot of a hypothetical situation or chain of events.

Schema: A data structure for knowledge representation. A method of presenting information about commonly occurring patterns of behavior. A means of organizing the data base of knowledge about a particular domain. A collection of observations, experiences, and reactions that are assumed to be always in effect. Frames and scripts are examples of schemas.

Scripts: A form of schema used for describing common sequences of events.

Search: The basic process involved in virtually all AI applications. To explore or examine in order to discover or learn something. To seek a particular object or goal.

Search Space: All of the attainable states (nodes) in an AI problem defined by a search tree or graph. Also called "state space."

Search Tree: A graph that looks like an inverted tree and is used to illustrate the search of all of the various alternatives in a search space. A hierarchical structure showing all of the goals and subgoals (nodes) interconnected by arcs discovered during the search process.

Semantic: Referring to the meaning, intention, or significance of a word, symbol, or expression.

Semantic Network: A method of knowledge representation using a graph comprising nodes and arcs where the nodes represent objects, situations, concepts, or entities and the arcs represent links describing the relationships between the nodes.

Shell: An expert system generator. A software package that allows you to create an expert system without programming.

Simulation: The process of having a computer mimic or imitate a physical or social system. A mathematical model implemented on a computer. Studying or designing a system or process by having the computer duplicate it.

Skeleton: A supporting structure or framework for creating an AI program. An expert system without the knowledge base. (See also "Shell.")

Slot: A sub-element of a frame or schema. A particular characteristic, specification, or definition used in forming a knowledge base. The name, definition, feature, or description of an attribute in a frame.

Smalltalk: A programming language developed at Xerox's Palo Alto Research Laboratory and useful in AI applications. Programming is viewed as a collection of objects that communicate with one another by passing messages.

Software: A general term describing a program or collection of programs used by a digital computer. Programs used to control and program the computer or applications programs that implement specific functions.

Speech Recognition: See "Voice recognition."

Supercomputer: The largest and fastest computers available, typically mainframes with superior operating speed and extensive data storage capability. Computers using the latest and most advanced technology to achieve superior performance in scientific and engineering computations. Computers with a speed of at least 20 MFLOPS but often in the 100 to 2000 MFLOPS range.

Syllogism: Deductive reasoning from the general to the specific. A method of deductive reasoning made up of a major premise, a minor premise, and a conclusion.

Symbol: One thing that represents something else by convention or association. A printed sign or designation used to represent some element, quantity, quality, or relationship in mathematics, logic, and computer programming.

Symbolic Computing: Using symbols rather than numbers to represent and manipulate facts, ideas, concepts, knowledge, and relationships in order to reason and understand.

Symbolic Logic: A formal system for calculus in which symbols are used to represent quantities and relationships for the purpose of reasoning and problem-solving.

Symbolic Manipulation: What all AI software does. Working with symbols that represent knowledge to reach a decision or solve a problem.

Thinking: The process of thought or reasoning. To formulate mentally. To decide, judge, consider, and otherwise reflect upon a subject.

Tool: A software package, such as an expert system shell, that makes it easier to create other software. Includes high-level languages such as LISP and Prolog.

Top-Down Reasoning: A structured method of working backward from a desired goal to determine subgoals and a path through the search tree that will yield a suitable solution to a problem. (See also "Backward-Chaining.")

Tree: A graph that resembles a tree with a root, branches, and leaves. A diagram made of nodes that represent objects, goals, or subgoals interconnected by arcs to form branches and leaves. A graphical system for defining a domain or search space.

Tree Search: The process of exploring or investigating a tree graph for the purpose of solving a problem or reaching a decision.

Trigger: The condition that exists in a rule-based system when all of the conditions of a rule are satisfied by the current situation. (See also "Fire.")

Turing Test: A test designed to determine if a machine has intelligence. An interrogator is separated from a person or a machine and communicates with that person or machine through a terminal. If, through a series of questions, the examiner cannot be certain whether he or she is communicating with a person or a machine, the machine is said to be intelligent or to be able to think.

Unification: A pattern-matching algorithm in which the mathematical expressions for the patterns are manipulated by substituting specific values for variables until they are identical.

User Interface: That portion of a computer program that communicates with the operator. A portion of the program that accepts inputs and generates outputs with such techniques as natural language and menus. (See also "Interface" and "Menu.")

VAX: A line of minicomputers made by Digital Equipment Corp. (DEC) and widely used in AI research and development.

Vision: See "Computer Vision."

VMS: An operating system developed by Digital Equipment Corp. (DEC) using virtual memory techniques on the VAX line of computers.

Voice Recognition: The process of having a computer or other electronic device recognize voice input from a user or operator. A system of picking up voice commands with a microphone, recognizing spoken words, and converting them into digital signals that can be processed by a digital computer and used for control purposes. The front-end of a natural language understanding system.

Wisdom: Knowing and understanding what is right or true. Good judgment and common sense combined with extensive learning. Awareness and knowledge based on education and experience.

Workstation: A computer, sometimes of the desktop variety, generally dedicated to a specific application, such as AI program development or computer-aided design. A computer system that assists the user and improves productivity.

XCON: An expert system developed jointly by Digital Equipment Corp. (DEC) and Carnegie-Mellon University and used to help configure VAX computer systems. Also called "R1."

Index

Answers to Quizzes

Chapter 1

1. b
2. d
3. a
4. c
5. a
6. c
7. d
8. a
9. b
10. d
11. c
12. d
13. c
14. a
15. b
16. c
17. d
18. b
19. c
20. a
21. c
22. b

Chapter 2

1. c
2. a
3. True
4. d
5. b
6. b
7. a
8. d
9. c
10. d
11. c
12. b
13. d
14. False
15. a
16. b
17. d
18. a
19. a
20. c

Chapter 3

1. b
2. c
3. a
4. d
5. d
6. d
7. a
8. a
9. c
10. d
11. b
12. a
13. b

Chapter 4

1. a
2. b
3. c
4. d
5. d
6. c
7. b
8. a
9. b
10. c
11. a
12. d
13. a
14. c
15. a
16. d
17. b
18. c
19. a
20. c

Chapter 5

1. b
2. a
3. d
4. c
5. c
6. b
7. a
8. d
9. b
10. d

Chapter 6

1. d
2. c
3. b
4. a
5. c
6. a
7. b
8. a
9. b
10. c
11. b
12. d
13. a
14. a
15. b
16. c
17. d
18. b
19. c
20. a

Chapter 7

1. d
2. a
3. b
4. c
5. c
6. d
7. a
8. c
9. d
10. b
11. a
12. b
13. d
14. a
15. c